How to make
Animations
for
lip reading practice

by Tony Edens

Surrey, England, 2016

Contents

1. Introduction

The purpose of this book is to enable the user to create film clips of moving lips primarily for practising lip reading.

This is done by creating animated GIF files of moving lips and embedding them in PowerPoint shows.

Any reference to movie clips or animations refers to this process only.

This book should be used in conjunction with the companion book "Lip Reading a self-help textbook".

This book will enable you to:

- Make movie clips of speaking lips for practising lip reading;
- To create movie clips of phrases used in the lip reading self-help textbook;
- To create movie clips of your own words and phrases;
- To combine your clips into PowerPoint repeating shows for your own lip reading practice.

This book will show you how to:

- Create your own library of lip shapes from the provided master copies;
- Create movie clips from provided lip shape sequences;
- Create lip shape sequences from your own words and phrases for making your own movie clips.

This book provides:

- A set of lip shape master copies for building your library of lip shapes;
- Step-by step instructions for creating the library;
- Step-by-step instructions for creating movie clips;
- Step-by-step instructions for creating a repeating PowerPoint show for lip reading practice;
- Lip shape sequence lists for the sets of practice phrases used in the companion book "Lip Reading a self-help textbook";
- Step by-step instructions for building movie clips of your own words and phrases.
- A trouble shooting section.
- Step-by step instructions for performing relevant tasks in GIF Animator and PowerPoint.

You will need:

- A means of copying images from the book into your personal computer. This is best done using the Kindle version of the book and the "Kindle for PC" app. downloadable from the Amazon website.
- A GIF animator program like "Easy GIF Animator";
- Microsoft PowerPoint or a similar program like Libre Office Impress.

The speaking lips animations:

The animations you will produce are called animated GIF files. GIF stands for Graphics Interchange Format. It was developed for use on internet pages and has two useful characteristics:

1. It can be used for moving images;
2. It can have a transparent background.

Your animated GIFs can be incorporated into PowerPoint shows as described in a later chapter or they could, if required, be used on web pages.

Animated GIFs are useful for short duration movie sequences and that is ideal for lip reading practice clips. You will also find that animated GIFs are fairly simple to modify to get a desired result.

The PowerPoint shows you produce can be set up to step though a given sequence of spoken phrases or sentences and to repeat the cycle indefinitely. They can also be scaled to fit a particular display screen or a particular viewing situation.

2. Creating a lip shape picture library

Moving pictures seen on film, television or computer screen are produced by displaying a sequence of still pictures one after another in quick succession. When it is done at the right speed, and with suitable still pictures, our brains interpret what is seen as a moving single image.

With a film or video recording of a moving scene the still photographs are shot, timed and ordered automatically.

When the still pictures are assembled artificially we call this animation.

The moving pictures we will create in this book are animations of speaking lips. They will be created from sequences of still pictures selected from a library of still pictures stored on your computer.

Before we can make any animations we need to create a library of still pictures on your computer. There needs to be one picture of each of the master copy images depicted in this book.

Creating the library needs to be done only once. But it needs to be done carefully, because any imperfection you produce at this stage will be reproduced in all your future animations.

Take a look at the master copies. You will see that there are 30 different images, each with its own name, and each inside a rectangular frame. The task is to copy these master images into separate files in your computer all having the same names as those given with the master copies.

You will need to do the following:

1. Create a new folder on your computer to contain all your images.

Using Windows Explorer, or a similar facility:

Navigate your way to where you want your new folder;

Click on the "New Folder" icon;

Choose a name for your folder – I suggest you call it "Lip Shapes".

2. Copy the master copies to your new folder.

To be able to do this you will need:

- A means of getting the master copies from the book into your computer. This is best done using the Kindle version of the book with the Kindle for PC App.
- To have a means of capturing a screen image – either a key marked "Print Screen" or similar. Alternatively

you could use a screen capture program like "MWSnap" which is downloadable from the internet.

- To have a GIF Animator program such as "GIF Animator" or "Easy GIF Animator" or something similar. The two listed are commercially available and are downloadable from the internet. Both offer free trial versions for you to try out before you buy.

I am using the Kindle version of the book on a Windows 10 computer that has a key marked "Print Screen". I am also using "Easy GIF Animator". My dialogue assumes that you are doing the same – so if you are not you will need to bear this in mind and will need to modify my instructions accordingly.

1. Display the first Master Image on your computer screen. Two images of each are provided – you should use the larger one. (Take note of whether you are displaying at 100% or some other zoom level – you will need to keep this the same every time you copy an image.)

2. Press "Print Screen". This copies the whole screen image to the clipboard.

3. Minimize or close the "Kindle for PC" App.

4. Open "Easy GIF Animator" and select the "Home" tab:

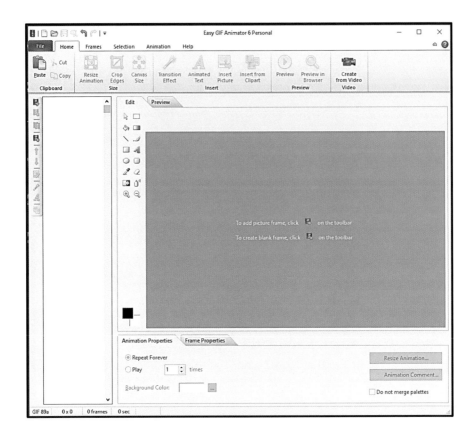

Click on "Paste" to copy the clipboard image into "Easy GIF Animator".

You will see part of your whole screen image in the "Easy GIF Animator" display (the display screen is not big enough to show it all).

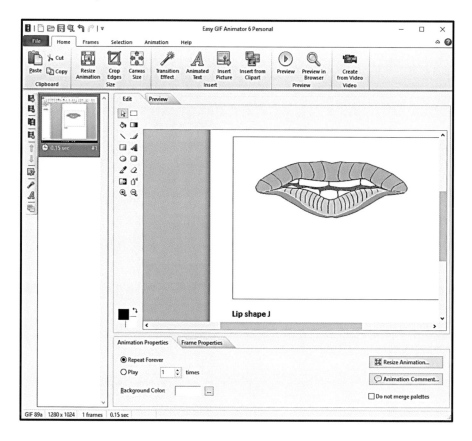

Click on the "Crop Edges" icon.

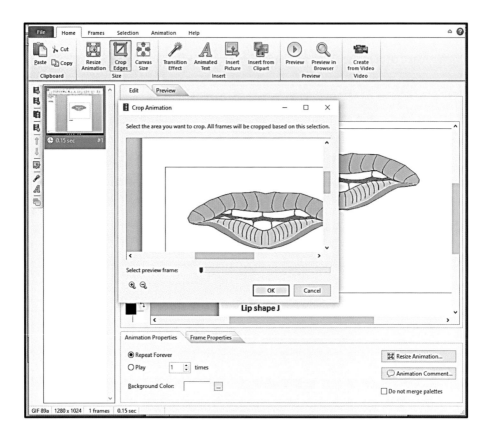

Using your mouse

*Move to the top left corner **of the picture frame.***

Hold the mouse key down.

*Move to the bottom right corner **of the picture frame.***

Release the mouse key.

When you are satisfied that you have accurately selected the area within the frame, *press OK.*

Easy GIF Animator will show the image you have selected.

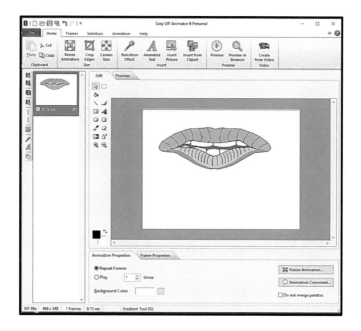

If you are happy with the result:

Click save and when prompted;

Choose an appropriate name and location for the new file.

The name should be the same as for the shape you are copying (in the example shown it is "J").

Easy GIF Animator will save it as a GIF image called in this case "J.gif".

You have now created the first item in your library of lip shapes. You now need to repeat the operation for each of the lip shapes contained in the collection of master copies in this book.

Modifying or tidying the library items

Once you have created and tested your library by creating an animation (Chapter 3) you may wish to make some changes. In my case I didn't want to see the frame around each picture I also wanted the background to be transparent.

Step-by-step instructions for doing this follow.

Other tasks you may wish to carry out are detailed in the "How to do things in In Easy GIF Animator" section.

To remove the frame from around the picture:

Open your lip shape file in Easy GIF Animator

Select the Edit tab:

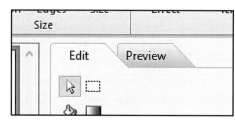

To select the foreground colour:

Click on the black square:

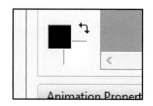

Click on the white square:

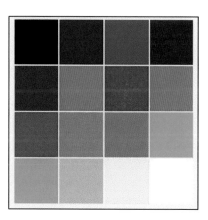

Select the paint brush icon:

Then paint over the bits you don't want.

To create a transparent background:

Select the Fill Tool icon:

Tick the fill with transparency box:

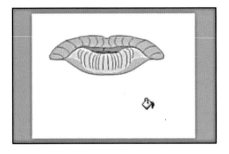

Then flood the background:

3. How to create animations of speaking lips

To create an animation you need to go through the following steps:

1. Obtain or create the lip shape text – I have taken my sample from the practice phrases in section 12 of this book.

It is:

[Pressure of work]M.r.e.j.y.uu.r.   o.v.   w.er.k.

"Pressure of work" is what the completed animation will say and will also be the name we give to the file containing the animation.

The letters following [Pressure of work] are the names of the lip shape pictures we need to assemble. They are separated from one another with full stops ".".

2. Assemble the lip shapes in the same order as follows:

Open Easy GIF Animator

Click on Create New Blank Animation

The screen changes to:

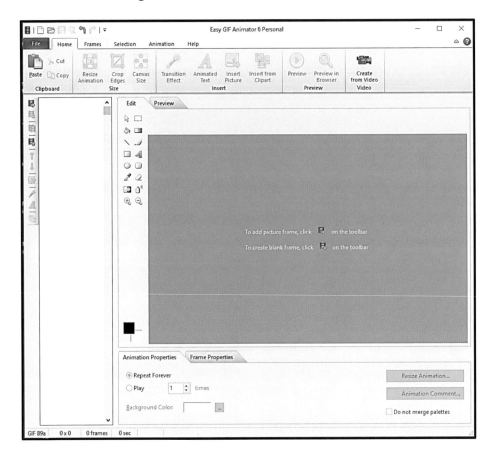

Click the insert icon:

(situated in the left margin of the display)

The "Open" dialogue appears:

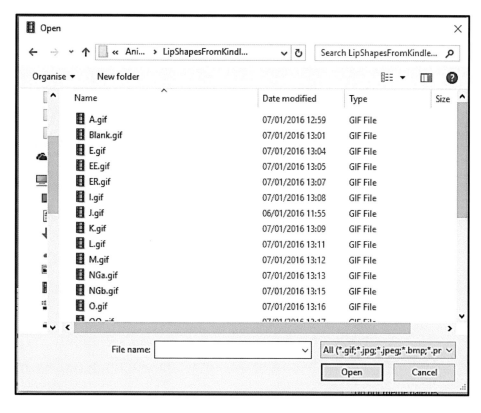

*Navigate to the folder **containing your lip shape collection.***

Select the desired shape .

Click on "Open".

The shape will appear in the Easy GIF Animator display:

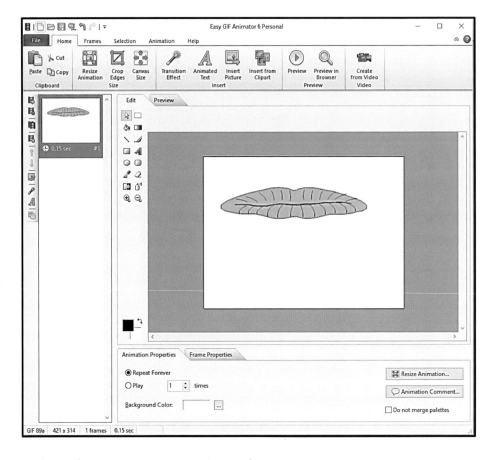

Select the Frame Properties tab:

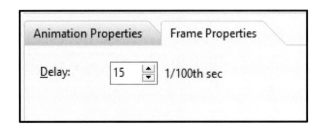

Choose Delay 15 1/100 th sec.

Then repeat the following for each of the listed lip shapes:

- *Click the insert icon*
- *Select the lip shape*
- *Press OPEN*

(Easy GIF Animator will remember where the lip shape collection is held – it will also remember the delay time)

3. Set the start and finish point for the animation.

When you have inserted all the lip shapes for "Pressure of work":

Insert "Lips at rest" picture – with a delay of 100 (1 second).

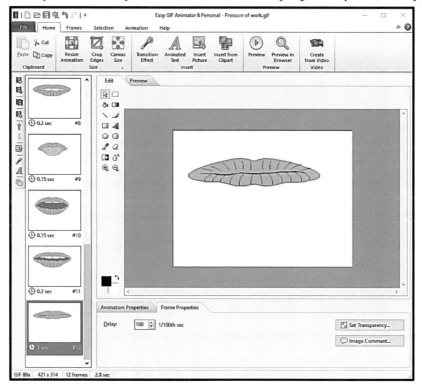

4. Separate the words:

Highlight in turn the last lip shape of each word and increase the delay from 15 to 20.

5. Set the repeat function:

Select the Animation Properties tab:

Select Repeat Forever:

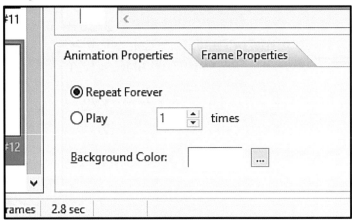

5. Test your animation.

Select Preview tab:

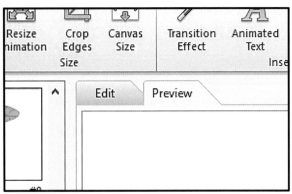

Click :

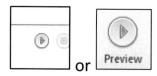 or

The lips will start to move and you should be able to see that they are saying "Pressure of work" over and over again with a short break between each.

You can stop it at any time by one doing of the following:

Click on the [◉] symbol;

Click on any one of your pictures;

Press one of the arrow keys on your computer keyboard.

To restart click on [▷ Preview]

6. Test run the sequence and modify delays to get the most natural speech rhythm.

7. Tidy up by modifying the 'lips at rest' delay time so that the animation takes a whole number of seconds. This will make it easier to incorporate your animation into a repeating PowerPoint show.

8. Save as "Pressure of work" in a different folder from your lip shape library.

4. How to create a repeating PowerPoint show

In the previous section we went through the process of creating a short movie clip (an animated GIF) from a provided list of lip shape names (lip shape text).
As you begin this chapter it is assumed that you have repeated the process several times and have now got a set of GIF animations stored in a folder on your PC.
I have built mine using the set of phrases taken from chapter 9 of the self-help textbook also listed in the Practice Phrases section of this book. They are stored in a folder called "Lip shape M phrases".

The folder contains:
Part and parcel.gif
Public speaking.gif
Mind over matter.gif
Broken Promises.gif
Pressure of work.gif
Pride of place.gif
Method in his madness.gif
Pass the parcel.gif

You will notice from the screen-shot that I have incorporated a file number and time into my file names. The use of a file number makes sure my files are always listed in the correct order as I work. The time in seconds I got from the Easy GIF Animator display – you will remember that I suggested you make your animations a complete number of seconds. This record of time the animation takes is included in the file name so that it is ready to hand when I need it as I build the PowerPoint show.

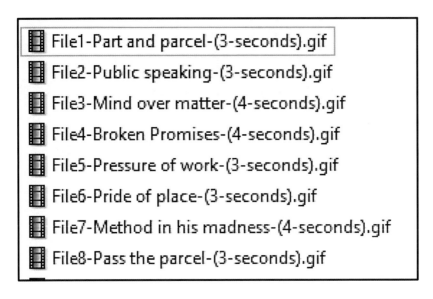

So by careful planning, the list of GIF animations contains the order they are arranged in, what the animations say, and how long each one takes.

We are now ready to start creating a PowerPoint Show. (I am using Microsoft PowerPoint 2010).

Open PowerPoint.

Create a new slide by clicking on the New Slide icon:

Click on the rectangle that says "Click to add text" and proceed to type in a list of your phrases.

The result is as follows:

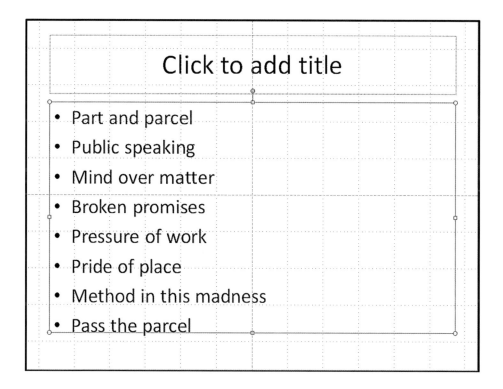

By clicking on the corner, and dragging the mouse resize the box to fit the list of phrases.

The screen will look like this:

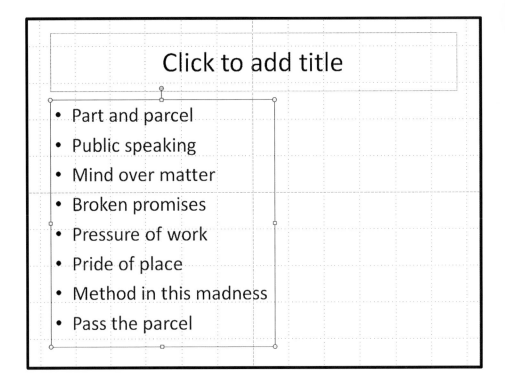

Next select the Insert tab. And click on Picture:

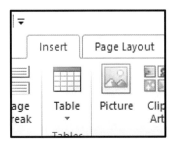

Navigate to your folder of GIF animations and select the first one:

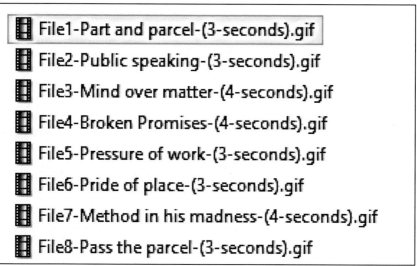

Click Insert:

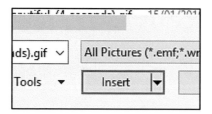

A still image will appear in the middle of the display:

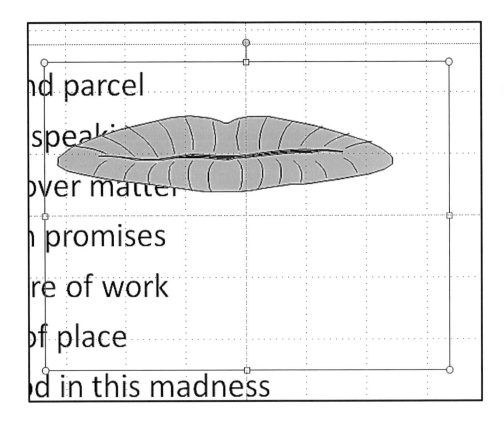

nd parcel

speak

over matter

n promises

re of work

of place

d in this madness

The picture is far too large and in the wrong place.

(In my library of lip shapes all the images have a transparent background so the words and, as you will shortly see, the colour behind the animation show through)

Click and drag the <u>corners</u> to re-size the picture.

Click and drag the <u>lines</u> to move the picture.

Giving this result:

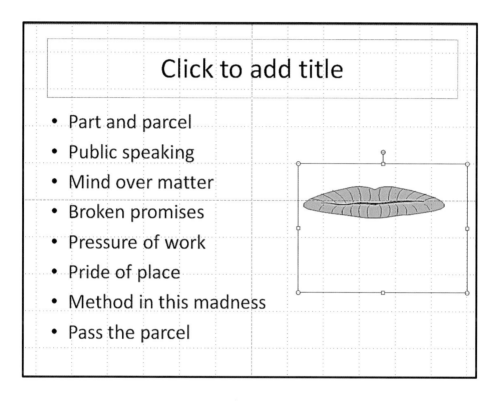

Now we can add the title:

Click on "Click to add title".

Type in your title:

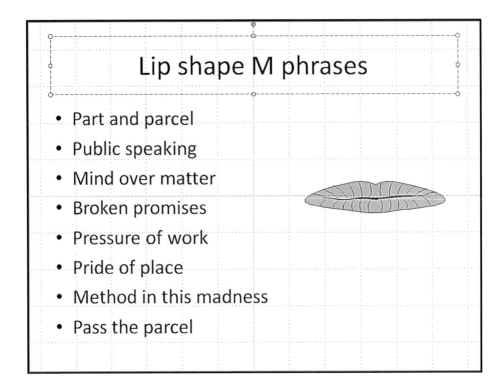

A plain white display is a bit boring so let's introduce a bit of colour:

Click on the Design tab:

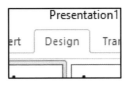

Click on Background styles:

Click on Format background:

Bringing you to this display:

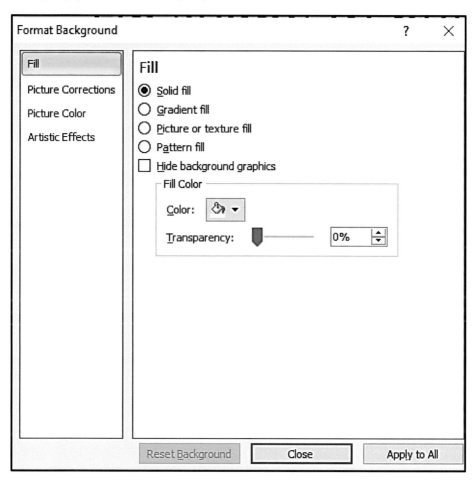

Click on "Color".

The following box will appear:

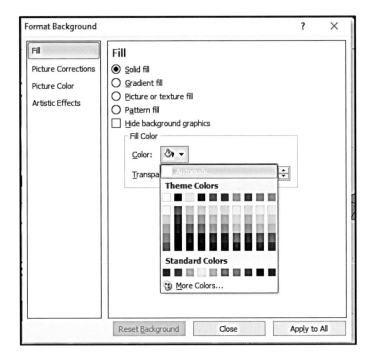

Choose your colour.

Click Apply to All.

This is the result:

Lip shape M phrases

- Part and parcel
- Public speaking
- Mind over matter
- Broken promises
- Pressure of work
- Pride of place
- Method in this madness
- Pass the parcel

When you are happy with your design it is time to test your animation.

Locate the tiny icons at the bottom right of the display – the highlighted one is for Edit mode and is the mode you are currently using – clicking the one on the right (a picture of a screen on a stand) will start the show. Right clicking your mouse (or pressing the Esc key) will stop the show:

Click the Screen icon and see what happens.

In my case the lips begin to move and appear to say "Part and parcel". I hope yours also works.

If your animation is not working refer to the trouble shooting section.

So far we have only one phrase in the PowerPoint show and can proceed to the next stage to add all our phrases.

To do this we will need to create a new slide for each of the phrases. We *could* do it by repeating everything we have just done, creating a new slide, typing the list of phrases, inserting the correct animated GIF, re-typing the title, etc. But that would be rather tedious – so we will do it by making copies of the frame we have already created and modifying the copies.

Before we do that there's one small change we need to make to the existing frame – that is to arrange for it to stop and move on after repeating the animation for a specified time. I suggest you use 24 seconds.

Click on the Transitions Tab :

In the Advance Slide section (top right of screen) select 24 seconds:

Why did I choose 24 seconds? Well, in the list of phrases we can see that some take 3 seconds and some take 4 seconds. I chose a period that would divide by 3 or by 4 and give a whole number. Twelve seconds would be a bit short so 24 seconds was chosen. This timing will be used in all the copies of the frame we make.

So let us go ahead and make the copies:

Click on the slide sorter icon:

The screen changes to:

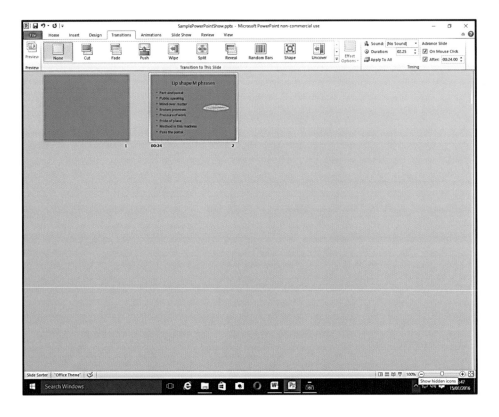

Slide Sorter mode shows several slides together allowing you to highlight, copy and paste them. It also allows you to delete them.

We have a blank slide that we don't need so we will delete it:

Click on the blank frame . The border changes showing that it has been selected.

Right click the mouse and select Delete slide.

You are now left with the slide containing your work and underneath is displayed 24 (the number of seconds it will be shown for).

Highlight the frame, and using right click, select Copy.

Now you can Paste a new copy simply by right clicking the mouse and selecting Paste from the list of options.

Do this seven times.

You should now have eight identical copies of your frame. Each will say the same phrase and each will be shown for 24 seconds.

But we want each one to say a different phrase and to indicate which phrase in the list it is saying by using italic type.

Switch to Normal mode:

Select the Home tab:

Go through your slides one by one, *highlight one of the phrases* in the list and *click the italic symbol.* A different phrase for each slide.

Next go through the slides one by one and change the picture to match the phrase in italic.

Highlight the picture.

Select the Format tab:

Click on Change Picture:

Navigate to the folder in which your GIF files are stored.

Highlight the one you want.

Click on Insert:

Move on to the next slide.

When all slides have their correct animations we finally need to make the slide show continuous:

Click on the Slide Show tab:

Click on the Set up slide show tool:

Put a tick in the Loop continuously box:

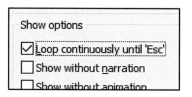

Click OK:

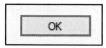

To make your PowerPoint a stand-alone show that will start automatically as soon as it is opened save it as a PowerPoint Show (.ppsx).

5. How to create animations of your own practice phrases

Chapter three of this book showed you how to create animated GIFs of phrases already encoded into lip shape text. This meant that the list and order of all the individual lip shapes had already been decided. If you want to animate your own lip reading practice phrases you will need to decide for yourself the choice and order of the component lip shapes and that is the subject of this chapter.

The job of creating the ordered list of lip shapes from a written text is in two stages:

1. Turn the written text into a list of sounds.
2. Turn the list of sounds into a list of lip shapes

This is equivalent to:

1. Turn the written text into phonetic text.
2. Turn the phonetic text into lip shape text.

Phonetic text and lip shape text are dealt with in the companion book "Lip reading – a self-help textbook" and some of the material is reproduced here in case you have not read the self-help textbook or for convenience of reference if you have.

We start with the written text, for example:

"Many hands make light work".

1. Turning the text into a list of sounds.

We next re-write it as it sounds by referring to the table below:

"Many hands make light work".

Becomes:

" M.e.n.ee.   H.a.n.z.   m.ay.k.   l.ii.t.   w.er.k."

(To keep them separate we put full-stops between the sounds)

Check the table to see if that is how you would say it. If not you can modify it to suit your speech patterns.

Table of Phonetic symbols and the sounds they represent:
Phonetic symbols are in bold type.

A as in hat	**N** as in nail
AH as in car	**NG** as in Thing
AIR as in care	**O** as in Hot
AW as in claw	**OH** as in Crow
AY as in hay	**OI** as in Boy
B as in box	**OO** as in Cool
C as in cat	**OW** as in Cow
CH as in choice	**P** as in Post
D as in dog	**Q** as in Queen
E as in tent	**R** as in Rat
EAR as in clear	**S** as in Silver
EE as in feet	**SH** as in Ship
ER as in hurt	**T** as in Tiger
EW as in few	**TH** as in thick
F as in Fig	**U** as in cup
G as in goat	**URE** as in pure
H as in hot	**UU** as in foot
I as in lip	**V** as in vast
IA as in idea	**W** as in wax
II as in cry	**X** as in box
J as in jam	**Y** as in year
L as in list	**Z** as in zoo
M as in make	**ZH** as in decision

2. Turning the list of sounds into a list of lip shapes.

So far we have converted conventional spelling:
"Many hands make light work".

Into phonetic spelling:
" M.e.n.ee. H.a.n.z. m.ay.k. l.ii.t. w.er.k."

To turn the sounds into lip shapes we refer to a second table as shown below. It then becomes:

"M.e.t.ee. k.a.t.z. m.e.ee.k. l.a.ee.t. w.er.k."

This is the list of lip shapes you will need to assemble to make your animated GIF.

You can now follow the instructions in section 3 to turn it into an animation and see if it really does say "Many hands make light work.

More information on phonetic and lip shape texts can be found in the companion book "Lip Reading – a self-help textbook".

Phonetic text to lip shape conversion table:

Phonetic Symbol	Lip Shape(s)	Phonetic Symbol	Lip Shape(s)
A	A	**N**	T
AH	A	**NG**	NG
AIR	E.ER	**O**	O
AW	UU	**OH**	O.OO
AY	E.EE	**OI**	UU.EE
B	M	**OO**	OO
C	K	**OW**	A.OO
CH	J	**P**	M
D	T	**Q**	W
E	E	**R**	R
EAR	EE.ER	**S**	S
EE	EE	**SH**	J
ER	ER	**T**	T
EW	EE.OO	**TH**	TH
F	V	**U**	U
G	K	**URE**	Y.UU.R
H	K	**UU**	UU
I	I	**V**	V
IA	EE.U	**W**	W
II	A.EE	**X**	S
J	J	**Y**	Y
K	K	**Z**	S
L	L	**ZH**	J
M	M		

6. Trouble shooting with Easy GIF Animator

Image doesn't move

    Cause: Easy Gif Animator working incorrectly.

    Solution: Select: *then:*

    Cause: There is only one picture in your animation.

    Solution: Add more pictures.

Image moves too quickly

    Cause: Delay times are too short.

    Solution: Increase the delay times of the pictures.

Image moves too slowly

    Cause: Delay times are too long.

    Solution: Reduce delay times of the pictures.

The lips make speaking movements but never pause

    Cause: The animation does not contain lips at rest.

    Solution: Add lips at rest lip shape at the end.

    Cause: Lips at rest has too short a delay time.

    Solution: Increase the delay time for this lip shape.

The words run together

    Cause: There is insufficient space between the words.

    Solution: Increase delays at word ends.

Lips say the right phrase but the movement looks wrong

    Cause: Some of the delay times are wrong.

    Solution: Experiment with different delay times.

The movement is nearly, but not quite, right

Cause: The animation contains wrong lip shapes.

Solution: Replace the incorrect images.

Cause: Lip shapes are in the wrong order   .

Solution: Change the lip shape order.

Cause: Some lip shapes are missing.

Solution: Identify and insert the missing images.

Lips say the wrong phrase

Cause: The GIF file name is wrong.

Solution: Change the file name to match the phrase.

Moving image flickers or moves about

Cause: Your library contains images that are incorrectly cropped or re-sized.

Solution: Correct the affected images.

Solution: Re-copy and re-crop from the master set.

Unwanted extra lines keep appearing

Cause: Your library contains image(s) that contain unwanted lines.

Solution: Rub out or paint over the unwanted parts of the library image.

7. Trouble shooting with PowerPoint

The lips don't move

Cause: You are not in Slide Show mode.

Solution: Select to enter Slide Show mode.

Cause: The GIF file is incorrect.
Solution: Check the file using Easy GIF Animator.

Cause: The GIF file is incorrectly named.
Solution: Rename the file so that the name ends with .gif.

The lips move then stop

Cause: The Repeat Forever option was not selected.
Solution: Check in Easy GIF Animator that Animation
Properties has Repeat Forever selected.

The show stops at the end and does not repeat

Cause: The Slide Show was not set to repeat.
Solution: In PowerPoint under the Slide Show tab put a
tick in the box labelled "Loop continuously until Esc."

The lips say the wrong phrase

Cause: The wrong GIF file has been copied onto the slide.
Solution: In PowerPoint, highlight the picture, select
Format then Change Picture, then select the correct
picture file.
Cause: The GIF file has the incorrect name.
Solution: Check and correct the file using Easy GIF
Animator

The words run together
Cause: The GIF file is incorrect.
Solution: Open the GIF file in Easy GIF Animator, locate the last lip shape of each word and increase the delay. In PowerPoint change the picture to the new version with increased delays.

It is not clear when the phrase starts and finishes
Cause: The GIF file is incorrect.
Solution: Use Easy GIF Animator to insert lips at rest at the end of the phrase with about 1 second delay. Reload the amended GIF file into the PowerPoint show.

The lips don't seem to say quite what you want
Cause: You have probably made a mistake when assembling your animation.
Solution: Use Easy GIF Animator to check and correct your GIF file. Then reload it into the PowerPoint show.

8. How to do things in In Easy GIF Animator

How to step through your animation sequences to:

- Check for unwanted lines or other marks
- Check for the correct lip shapes
- Check if the order is correct

Open your animation in Easy GIF Animator.

Click on any of the small images in the left hand column to highlight it and make it appear in the large window.

The display below shows the animation produced in chapter three. I have highlighted lip shape V and lip shape V is now displayed in the large window.

A number of unwanted lines kept flickering on and off in the animation and I can now see that they are on this picture of lip shape V, so I can now go ahead and delete them.

If I highlight the sequence of pictures one by one I can step through the sequence to spot where there is a mistake – you generally see that there is a mistake when you run the animation but can't pin-point whereabouts in the sequence it is. By stepping through it is much easier to pin-point where the mistake is.

Lip shape V is selected:

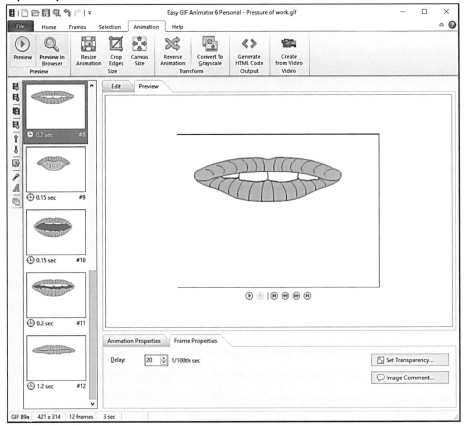

How to change delay times

Select and display the frame you want to change.

Select the Frame Properties tab:

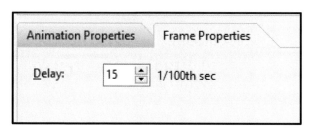

Modify the number in the box (this is the number of hundredths of a second the picture will be shown).

Click SAVE when done.

How to remove unwanted lines or other marks

Open the lip shape file in Easy GIF Animator.

Select the Edit tab:

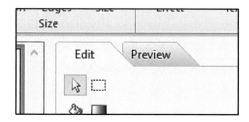

Change the foreground colour

from 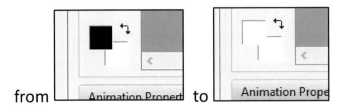 to

(see: *How to colour or shade a lip shape picture*)

Select the paint brush icon:

Then paint over the bits you don't want.

Click SAVE when done.

How to create a transparent background
Select the paint pot icon:

Tick the fill with transparency box:

☑ Fill with Transparency

Then flood the background:

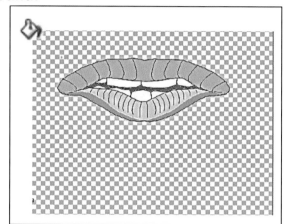

Click SAVE when done.

How to remove a lip shape
Highlight the frame showing the unwanted lip shape.

Click the Delete icon:

or press the Delete key.

Click SAVE when done.

How to insert a lip shape

Click the Insert icon:

 (left hand column)

Navigate to the required lip shape:

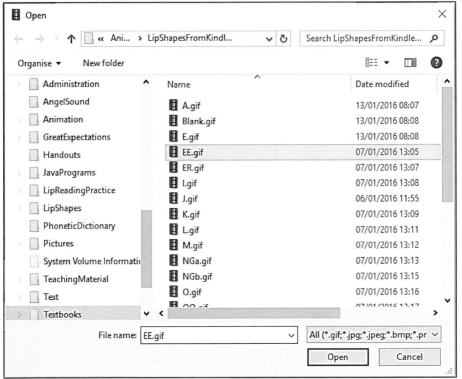

Highlight it and click on Open.

The new lip shape will appear <u>at the end of your sequence of lip shapes.</u>

You can now move it to its new position.
Click SAVE when done.

How to move a lip shape

Highlight the image you want to move:

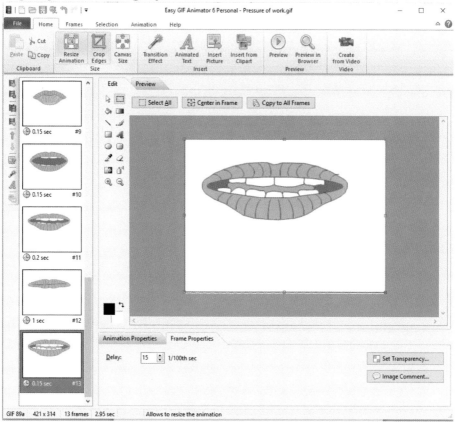

Click on the arrow keys ⬆ or ⬇ *(left hand column) to move the picture up or down in the sequence.*

Click SAVE when done.

How to copy a lip shape

Highlight the lip shape you want to copy

Click Copy:

*Highlight the lip shape **after which the copy is to be placed.***

Click on Paste:

Click SAVE when done.

_____

How to colour or shade a lip shape picture

With your lip shape picture displayed in the large window:

Select the Edit Tab:

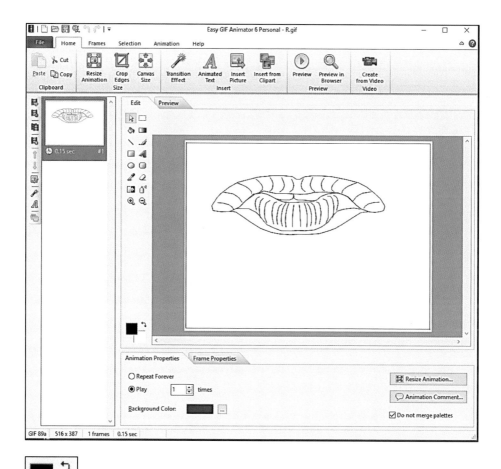

Shows the colours Easy GIF Animator is using .

In this case it is black for the foreground and white for the background.

Click on the foreground colour (black square):

This brings you to the "Color Picker":

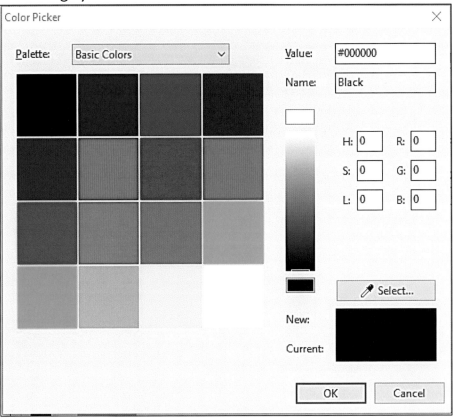

Click on the red square:
Another box on the display changes

 *from*  *to*

You can change the colour shown as "New" by clicking on a different coloured square and by moving the slider on the right:

When "New" shows the desired colour click on "OK".
This brings you back to the main display where you will see that the foreground colour indicator shows your chosen colour:

To colour any area of the picture:
Select the "Fill" tool :

Your cursor takes on the same shape.

Click on the area you want to colour.

How to match colours exactly

The colour picker is a very useful tool for matching colours. Let us say that you have gone to some trouble to getting just the right shade of red for the lips in your picture and you want to reproduce that exact colour on all the lip shape pictures in your library. So starting from the situation where you have a library of uncoloured lip shape pictures and just one of them with the correct lip colour. Carry out this procedure using Easy GIF Animator:

Open the correctly coloured picture (in my case lip shape L).

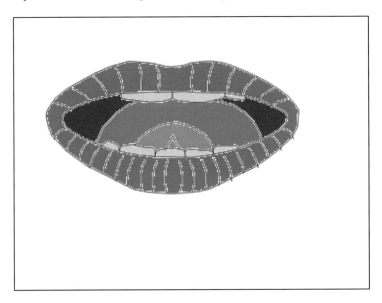

Click on the colour picker icon:

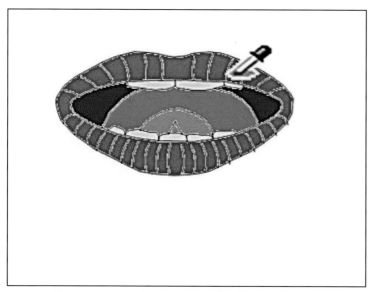

Carry the colour picker icon to the colour you want:

Click the mouse.

The colour indicator will change

From 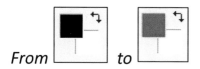 *to*

Save your picture (if you wish)

Click Open and select an uncoloured picture:

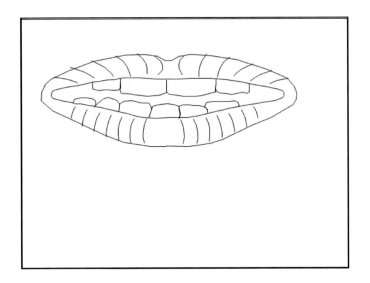

You will see that the foreground colour is still set to:

Use the Fill Tool to flood the area with colour:

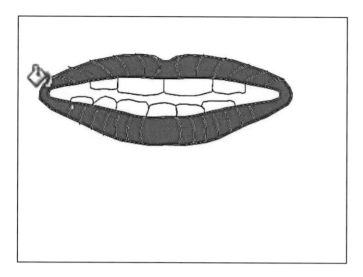

Save the picture.

Proceed to Open, colour and save all your pictures in turn.

Repeat this procedure for each of the special colours used in your pictures. Doing it this way avoids mis-match of colours leading to flickering animations.

How to set an animation to repeat indefinitely

Select the Animation Properties tab:

Select Repeat Forever:

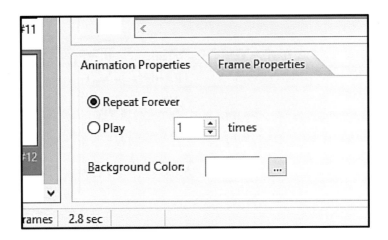

Click SAVE when done.

---

9. How to do things in PowerPoint

How to make a PowerPoint show repeat indefinitely

Click on the Slide Show tab:

Click on the Set up slide show tool:

Put a tick in the Loop continuously box:

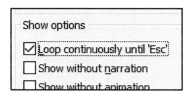

Click OK:

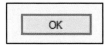

How to replace a picture in PowerPoint
Highlight the picture you want to replace
Click on the Picture Tools Format tab:

then select change picture:

Navigate to the new picture.
Click to select it.
Click on Insert.

How to modify animated phrases
You cannot modify the animated GIF files in PowerPoint.
You need to do this in Easy GIF Animator. Once that has been
done you can use PowerPoint to replace the picture in the
PowerPoint show.

How to change when to move to the next PowerPoint slide

With the slide displayed in Normal Mode:

Select the Transitions Tab.:

In the Advance Slide box:
Make sure the boxes are ticked
Change the number (seconds) to the
new value

How to stop the PowerPoint show
You can stop a PowerPoint show by doing one of the following:
- Press the ESC key.
- Right click the mouse and select "End Show".
- Press the - (hyphen) key.
- Press Ctrl. + Break key.

How to start the PowerPoint show
Click on the Slide Show icon at the bottom right if the screen:

Alternatively you can press the F5 key.

How to change the order of the PowerPoint slides

Select Slide Sorter mode by clicking the icon at the bottom right of the screen:

Once in Slide Sorter mode you can drag and drop the slides you want to move (click and hold the mouse over the slide, still holding the mouse key move the cursor to the place you want to put the slide then release the mouse key.)
In Slide Sorter mode you can also copy and paste slides and also delete slides.

---

10. How to do things in Windows

How to change the name of a GIF file

On Windows desktop:

Double click the "This PC" or "My Computer" icon.

Navigate to the file you want to rename.

Highlight it:

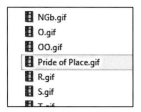

Right click the mouse:

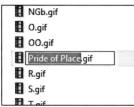

Type in the new name:

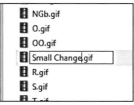

Press the return key.

How to create a new folder

On Windows desktop:

Double click the "This PC" or "My Computer" icon.

Navigate to the place where you want your new folder.

Click on the "New Folder" tool:

The new folder appears at the bottom of the list:

Type in a name for your new folder:

Press the Return key.

---

11. Discovering the words

In some ways we humans are a clever lot. There's a whole range of things we can do better than other members of the animal kingdom. We can't fly like a bird or run like some of our four legged friends but when it comes to communication by talking we win hands down. Then, not all that long ago, someone invented the computer. And it was not long before we found that a lot of the tasks we had a pride in performing could be done faster and maybe better by the computer.

One little experiment done at the University of East Anglia in 2009 set a computer the task of lip reading. Now some of us humans have a bit of trouble when it comes to lip reading silent lips in a lip reading class and I for one would have hoped that when a computer had a go it would also encounter a problem. But that was not to be. The computer beat us humans hands down as they say.

In the experiment volunteers were filmed as they said a series of single words. The film was of the whole face encompassing mouth, nose, eyes, chin, hair and everything else within the face outline. The sound track was removed from the film which was then played back, to a computer programmed to lip read, and to a group of people who, so far as I know, hadn't had any formal lip reading training. The result was that the computer managed to correctly lip read 80% of the words while the people set the same task managed to score only 32%.

I am not at all surprised that people scored only 32% as it is often quoted that only about 30% of the verbal information in speech is visible to the lip reader but I was surprised that the computer managed to get such a high score.

But the story doesn't end there because the experimenters went further. They repeated the experiment comparing human scores to the computer scores. This time showing only the area around the speaker's mouth. It comes as no surprise to find that the computer score was unchanged. It still managed to lip read 80% of the words while people scored even less than before.

Then the experimenters tried other variations by tracing from the film just the outlines of face, eyes, nose and mouth and showing just the outlines to the computer and lip reading volunteers.

The results were that using outlines of the whole face the computer scored 80% and again when showed only outlines of the mouth and lips the computer's score was still unchanged.

So what can we learn from the experiment and why the disparity of scores between human and computer?

First let's think about the differences between a lip reading computer "brain" and a human brain. The human brain, like the brains of other creatures, is a parallel device – that is that its various parts can work independently of each other, and at the same time, whereas the computer is a serial device that does its tasks one at a time and at very high speed.

What appears to be the case in the experiment is that the computer was set up to simulate a neural network so that it could behave like the human brain. The panels below summarise the differences between them.

The high speed of the electronic computer compared to the rather sluggish rate of operation of the biological human brain means that even when having to do things sequentially the computer can still compete well in single tasks like lip reading, and its small number of neurons is adequate for the lip reading task. But the human brain has a lot of other things to do while it is lip reading – most particularly arranging the wellbeing of the whole body. If any of the essential body functions stop the whole body dies so the brain is busy in the background keeping things going. If we don't sense and avoid danger, harm could ensue or even death so the brain is in constant watch. I must say that I find that my brain almost has a mind of its own and is not really under my conscious control. Things that we would like to forget, we cannot forget and the brain hangs onto the most unpleasant memories – the more traumatic the experience the less willing the brain is to let us forget. I think this must be part of the brain's survival strategy developed over the millions of years of its evolution. If primitive man had been allowed to admire the scenery and ignore the sabre-toothed tiger creeping up on him he would not have survived and we would not be here. So as soon as the brain senses something out of the ordinary it seizes your attention. Never mind about the task in hand, lip reading or whatever else it was, this is survival and your brain makes sure that it has your immediate attention.

Computer brain	Human brain
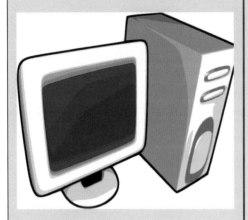	
• *High speed*	• *Low speed*
• *Narrow range of tasks*	• *Wide range of tasks*
• *Small number of neurons*	• *Large number of neurons*
• *Doesn't get tired or bored*	• *Gets tired and bored*
• *Doesn't get distracted*	• *Easily distracted*
• *The product of technical innovation*	• *The product of*

Getting back to the lip reading experiment, the human score dropped off when the face was obscured and only the lips were visible. Why? I think this must have been because the brain saw the obscured face as something unusual that required immediate attention. So attention was taken from the lip reading task to concentrate on an unusual situation. I personally find that when I am trying to lip read, my score goes down if there is anything unusual happening. If I'm in a lip reading class and someone comes in late my score goes down. If there's noise outside, my score goes down and if the teacher suddenly starts finger spelling, my score goes down. So that is probably the reason why the lip reading people scored less when everything other than the lips was obscured. The computer, on the other hand, is not programmed in this way. It is not easily distracted from the task in hand. It will keep working on the task in hand until it is made to stop.

Why was the computer's score higher than the human's? My guess would be that it is down to the computer's high speed of processing. The computer appears to have been able to pick up clues that the humans missed. We all know that the P B and M sounds all look alike to the lip reader but there are subtle differences that I can feel when I am saying them so possibly the computer was able to see those slight differences as the high speed film was replayed to it. It's nice to know the visual clues are there so maybe with lots of practice and close observation I may be able to spot some of them and improve my lip reading skills.

Where is the linguistic information? I find it surprising that the computer's score was 80% for every one of the tests reported. I've done enough scientific investigations to know that one rarely gets precisely the same score every time a test is done – so I suspect that the figures have been rounded and simplified for us and that the actual scores obtained were, on average, not significantly different from 80%. By obscuring areas of the scene and by taking away the texture and colour of the film images to leave only the outlines of mouth and lips, leads to the conclusion that the computer used only the outlines of mouth and lips to do its lip reading and we are obliged to conclude that the linguistic information contained in the film of people lip speaking was contained in the outlines of mouth and lips and (probably) nowhere else. I would go a little further because I find from experiments using animated line drawings that it is perfectly feasible for people to lip read these images once they have got used to the novelty of viewing only the mouth and lips. So my belief is that the verbal information is present not just in the line drawings of the outlines of mouth and lips but particularly in the temporal information as one lip shapes gives way for another in succession. I also find that users of my system have no difficulty when they stop viewing animated line drawings for lip reading practice and start lip reading for real outside the classroom.

The moral of the story seems to be:

If you want the words (verbal information) – look at the lips.

If you want to read mood and emotions (non-verbal information) - look at the facial expressions and body language.

If you are practising your lip reading skills it's ok to use animated line drawn images.

- **To read emotions concentrate on the whole face and the body language.**

- **To get the best of both worlds look at the face and body language as you approach but look at the lips as soon as the conversation begins.**

- **To get the words concentrate on the lips.**

- **To practise your lip reading skills concentrate on the lips.**

12. Practice phrases from the textbook

Note that the text [in brackets] is what the lips will say when the animation is created. It is also the suggested file name for the animation.

The text following the bracketed title is the series of lip shape pictures you will need to assemble for the animation.

Chapter 9 - Lip Shape M
[Part and parcel]M.a.t.   a.t.t.   m.a.s.e.l.
[Public speaking]M.u.m.l.i.k.   s.m.ee.k.i.ng.
[Mind over matter]M.a.ee.t.t.   o.oo.v.er.   m.a.t.er.
[Broken Promises]M.r.o.oo.k.t.   M.r.o.m.i.s.i.s.
[Pressure of work]M.r.e.j.y.uu.r.   o.v.   w.er.k.
[Pride of place]M.r.a.ee.t.   o.v.   m.l.e.ee.s.
[Method in his madness]M.e.th.o.t.   i.t.   k.i.s.   m.a.t.t.e.s.
[Pass the parcel]M.a.s.   th.u.   m.a.s.e.l.
[Peculiar practice]M.e.k.ee.oo.l.ee.er.   m.r.a.k.t.i.s.
[Bus pass]M.u.s.   m.a.s.
[First past the post]V.er.s.t.   m.a.s.t.   th.u.   m.o.oo.s.t.
[Market prices]M.a.k.e.t.   m.r.a.ee.s.i.s.
[Bread and butter]M.r.e.t.   a.t.t.   m.u.t.er.
[Bright and beautiful]M.r.a.ee.t.   a.t.t.   m.ee.oo.t.i.v.uu.l.

Chapter 10 - Lip shape V
[Fast and furious]V.a.s.t.   a.t.t.   v.y.uu.r.ee.u.s.
[Fact and fiction]V.a.k.t.   a.t.t.   v.i.k.j.u.t.
[Few and far between]V.ee.oo.   a.t.t.   v.a.   m.e.t.w.ee.t.
[Halfway through]K.a.v.w.e.ee.   th.r.oo.
[Work of fiction]W.er.k.   o.v.   v.i.k.j.u.t.

[Frequent service]V.r.ee.w.t.t. s.er.v.i.s.
[Self service checkout]S.e.l.v. s.er.v.i.s. j.e.k.a.oo.t.
[Flight of fancy]V.l.a.ee.t. o.v. v.a.t.s.ee.
[Photo finish]V.o.oo.t.o.oo. v.i.t.i.j.
[A laugh a minute]U. l.a.v. u. m.i.t.i.t.
[That's enough]TH.a.t.s. e.t.u.v.
[Rough justice]R.u.v. j.u.s.t.i.s.

Chapter 11 - Lip shape W

[Quick on the draw]W.i.k. o.t. th.u. t.r.uu.
[Well wisher]W.e.l. w.i.j.er.
[Man and wife]M.a.t. a.t.t. w.a.ee.v.
[Quick brew up]W.i.k. m.r.oo. u.m.
[Crown Jewels]K.r.a.oo.t. J.ee.oo.e.l.s.
[Town crier]T.a.oo.t. k.r.a.ee.er.
[Brown as a berry]M.r.a.oo.t. a.s. u. m.e.r.ee.
[Long frown]L.o.ng. v.r.a.oo.t.
[Blustery shower]M.l.u.s.t.er.ee. j.a.oo.er.
[Wednesday week]W.e.t.s.t.e.ee. w.ee.k.
[Stone wall]S.t.o.oo.t. w.uu.l.
[Show business]J.o.oo.w. m.i.s.t.e.s.
[Borrowed time]M.o.r.o.oo.t. t.a.ee.m.
[Mow down]M.o.oo. t.a.oo.t.

Chapter 13 - Lip shape L
[Light work]L.a.ee.t. w.er.k.
[Earn a living]ER.t. u. l.i.v.i.ng.
[A living wage]U. l.i.v.i.ng. w.e.ee.j.
[Lost for words]L.o.s.t. v.uu. w.er.t.s.
[A level playing field]U. l.e.v.l. m.l.e.ee.i.ng. v.ee.l.t.
[Silver spoon]S.i.l.v.er. s.m.oo.t.
[Silver lining]S.i.l.v.er. l.a.ee.t.i.ng.

[Flight of fancy]V.l.a.ee.t.   o.v.   v.a.t.s.ee.
[Jolly good]J.o.l.ee.   k.uu.t.
[Silver collection]S.i.l.v.er.   k.o.l.e.k.j.u.t.
[Jolly careful]J.o.l.ee.   k.e.er.v.uu.l.
[College work]K.o.l.i.j.   w.er.k.
[College place   ]K.o.l.i.j.   m.l.e.ee.s.
[Smooth as silk]S.m.oo.th.   a.s.   s.i.l.k.
[Travelling salesman]T.r.a.v.e.l.i.ng.   s.e.ee.l.s.m.u.t.
[A silky texture]U.   s.i.l.k.ee.   t.e.s.j.y.uu.r.
[Travel card]T.r.a.v.l.   k.a.t.
[Labour of love]L.e.ee.m.er.   o.v.   l.u.v.
[Large as life]L.a.j.   a.s.   l.a.ee.v.
[University challenge]Y.oo.t.i.v.er.s.i.t.ee.   j.a.l.e.t.j.

Chapter 14 - Lip shape A
[Taking part]T.e.ee.k.i.ng.   m.a.t.
[Common market]K.o.m.u.t.   m.a.k.e.t.
[Last chance]L.a.s.t.   j.a.t.s.
[Crab apple tree]K.r.a.m.   a.m.l.   t.r.ee.
[Land of the free]L.a.t.t.   o.v.   th.u.   v.r.ee.
[Grand design]K.r.a.t.t.   t.e.s.a.ee.t.
[As quick as you can]A.s.   w.i.k.   a.s.   y.oo.   k.a.t.
[Hand over hand]K.a.t.t.   o.oo.v.er.   k.a.t.t.
[First past the post]V.er.s.t.   m.a.s.t.   th.u.   m.o.oo.s.t.
[He who laughs last]K.ee.   k.oo.   l.a.v.s.   l.a.s.t.
[Garden party]K.a.t.e.t.   m.a.t.ee.
[Part and parcel]M.a.t.   a.t.t.   m.a.s.e.l.
[Panic attack]M.a.t.i.k.   a.t.a.k.
[Cash in the bank]K.a.j.   i.t.   th.u.   m.a.ng.k.

Chapter 15 - Lip shape E

[Ever decreasing circles.]E.v.er. t.e.k.r.ee.s.i.ng. s.er.k.l.s..

[Evergreen bush]E.v.er.k.r.ee.t. m.u.j.

[Lemon marmalade]L.e.m.u.t. m.a.m.a.l.e.ee.t.

[Silver shred marmalade]S.i.l.v.er. j.r.e.t. m.a.m.a.l.e.ee.t.

[Leicester city]L.e.s.t.er. s.i.t.ee.

[Incredible price]I.t.k.r.e.t.i.m.l. m.r.a.ee.s.

[Better price]M.e.t.er. m.r.a.ee.s.

[Bread pudding]M.r.e.t. m.uu.t.i.ng.

[Heading for victory]K.e.t.i.ng. v.uu. v.i.k.t.uu.r.ee.

[Yellow fever]Y.e.l.o.oo. v.ee.v.er.

[Credit rating]K.r.e.t.i.t. r.e.ee.t.i.ng.

[Every man for himself]E.v.r.ee. m.a.t. v.uu. k.i.m.s.e.l.v.

[Holiday let]K.o.l.i.t.e.ee. l.e.t.

[Post a letter]M.o.oo.s.t. u. l.e.t.er.

[Bread and butter]M.r.e.t. a.t.t. m.u.t.er.

[Off to bed]O.v. t.oo. m.e.t.

Chapter 16 - Lip shape O

[Clock watching]K.l.o.k. w.o.j.i.ng.

[Cross words]K.r.o.s. w.er.t.s.

[Dream topping]T.r.ee.m. t.o.m.i.ng.

[Well trodden]W.e.l. t.r.o.t.e.t.

[Shocking story]J.o.k.i.ng. s.t.uu.r.ee.

[Win the lottery]W.i.t. th.u. l.o.t.er.ee.

[Daylight robbery]T.ail.a.ee.t. r.o.m.er.ee.

[Top dog]T.o.m. t.o.k.

[Office job]O.v.i.s. j.o.m.

[Good offer]K.uu.t. o.v.er.

[Stop the rot]S.t.o.m. th.u. r.o.t.

[Shop till you drop]J.o.m. t.i.l. y.oo. t.r.o.m.

[Climb to the top]K.l.a.ee.m. t.oo. th.u. t.o.m.

[Shot in the dark]J.o.t. i.t. th.u. t.a.k.

Chapter 17 - Lip shape K
[All that glitters]UU.l.   th.a.t.   k.l.i.t.er.s.
[More haste less speed]M.uu.   k.e.ee.s.t.   l.e.s.   s.m.ee.t.
[Grab some lunch]K.r.a.m.   s.u.m.   l.u.t.j.
[Cost of living]K.o.s.t.   o.v.   l.i.v.i.ng.
[Crazy idea]K.r.e.ee.s.ee.   a.ee.t.ee.u.
[Ice cream cornet]A.EE.s.   k.r.ee.m.   k.uu.t.i.t.
[Practical joke]M.r.a.k.t.i.k.a.l.   j.o.oo.k.
[Kind hearted man]K.a.ee.t.t.   k.a.t.e.t.   m.a.t.
[Clever child]K.l.e.v.er.   j.a.ee.l.t.
[Christmas cake]K.r.i.s.m.us k.e.ee.k.
[Sticky wicket]S.t.i.k.ee.   w.i.k.e.t.
[Garden gate]K.a.t.e.t.   k.e.ee.t.
[Comfortable seat]K.u.m.v.t.u.m.l.   s.ee.t.
[Credit card]K.r.e.t.i.t.   k.a.t.

Chapter 18 - Lip shape TH
[Thick and thin]TH.i.k.   a.t.t.   th.i.t.
[Thought provoking]TH.uu.t.   m.r.o.v.o.oo.k.i.ng.
[Cold weather]K.o.oo.t.   w.e.th.er.
[Weather station]W.e.th.er.   s.t.e.ee.j.u.t.
[Great North Road]K.r.e.ee.t.   T.uu.th.   R.o.oo.t.
[Withheld information]W.i.th.k.e.l.t.   i.t.v.uu.m.e.ee.j.u.t.
[Rather good]R.a.th.er.   k.uu.t.
[Food for thought]V.oo.t.   v.uu.   th.uu.t.
[Think about it]TH.i.ng.k.   u.m.a.oo.t.   i.t.
[Leather boots]L.e.th.er.   m.oo.t.s.
[Needle and thread]T.ee.t.l.   a.t.t.   th.r.e.t.
[Brother and sister]M.r.u.th.er.   a.t.t.   s.i.s.t.er.
[This and that]TH.i.s.   a.t.t.   th.a.t.
[Next month]T.e.s.t.   m.u.t.th.

Chapter 19 - Lip shape T

[Danger money]T.e.ee.t.j.er. m.u.t.ee.

[Do or die]T.oo. uu. t.a.ee.

[The devil's in the detail]TH.u. t.e.v.l.s. i.t. th.u.
t.ee.t.e.ee.l.

[Never a dull word]T.e.v.er. u. t.u.l. w.er.t.

[Dry cleaning]T.r.a.ee. k.l.ee.t.i.ng.

[Dark deed]T.a.k. t.ee.t.

[Duty bound]T.ee.oo.t.ee. m.a.oo.t.t.

[Drink and drive]T.r.i.ng.k. a.t.t. t.r.a.ee.v.

[National scandal]T.a.j.t.u.l. s.k.a.t.t.uu.l.

[TV drama]T.EE.V.EE. t.r.a.m.u.

[Never say die]T.e.v.er. s.e.ee. t.a.ee.

[Window shopping]W.i.t.t.o.oo. j.o.m.i.ng.

[Can't stop]K.a.t.t. s.t.o.m.

[Burnt fingers]M.er.t.t. v.i.ng.k.er.s.

[Stop and start]S.t.o.m. a.t.t. s.t.a.t.

[Point of view]M.uu.ee.t.t. o.v. v.ee.oo.

Chapter 20 - Lip shape R

[Wrong turning]R.o.ng. t.er.t.i.ng.

[Rise and Shine]R.a.ee.s. a.t.t. J.a.ee.t.

[Rover ticket]R.o.oo.v.er. t.i.k.i.t.

[River crossing]R.i.v.er. k.r.o.s.i.ng.

[Sour cream]S.a.oo.er. k.r.ee.m.

[Rhyme and reason]R.a.ee.m. a.t.t. r.ee.s.t.

[Really cheap]R.ee.u.l.ee. j.ee.m.

[Carried along]K.a.r.i.t. u.l.o.ng.

[Sorry story]S.o.r.ee. s.t.uu.r.ee.

[No problem]T.o.oo. m.r.o.m.l.e.m.

[Practical Joke]M.r.a.k.t.i.k.a.l. J.o.oo.k.

[Profit and loss]M.r.o.v.i.t. a.t.t. l.o.s.

[Cradle to grave]K.r.e.ee.t.l.   t.oo.   k.r.e.ee.v.
[Travel card]T.r.a.v.l.   k.a.t.

Chapter 21 - Lip shape S
[Is that wise]I.s.   th.a.t.   w.a.ee.s.
[Sudden movement]S.u.t.t.   m.oo.v.m.e.t.t.
[Press report]M.r.e.s.   r.e.m.uu.t.
[Excessive moisture]E.s.e.s.i.v.   m.uu.ee.s.j.er.
[New tricks]T.ee.oo.   t.r.i.k.s.
[No flies on him]T.o.oo.   v.l.a.ee.s.   o.t.   k.i.m.
[Taking possession]T.e.ee.k.i.ng.   m.o.oo.s.e.j.u.t.
[Fast food]V.a.s.t.   v.oo.t.
[Extra chips]E.s.t.r.u.   j.i.m.s.
[Slippery surface]S.l.i.m.er.ee.   s.er.v.i.s.
[Nuisance calls]T.ee.oo.s.u.t.s.   k.uu.l.s.
[An exact science]A.t.   e.s.a.k.t.   s.a.ee.e.t.s.
[Sealed lips]S.ee.l.t.   l.i.m.s.
[Exact amount]E.s.a.k.t.   u.m.a.oo.t.t.

Chapter 22 - Lip shape J
[Sugar free]J.uu.k.er.   v.r.ee.
[Cherry picking]J.e.r.ee.   m.i.k.i.ng.
[Service charge]S.er.v.i.s.   j.a.j.
[Lock up garage]L.o.k.   u.m.   k.a.r.i.j.
[Treasure trove]T.r.e.j.y.uu.r.   t.r.o.oo.v.
[Pleasure park]M.l.e.j.y.uu.r.   m.a.k.
[Life of leisure]L.a.ee.v.   o.v.   l.e.j.y.uu.r.
[Share and share alike]J.e.er.   a.t.t.   j.e.er.   u.l.a.ee.k.
[Bird watching]M.er.t.   w.o.j.i.ng.
[Precision engineering]M.r.e.s.i.j.u.t.   e.t.j.i.t.ee.r.i.ng.
[Nuclear fission]T.ee.oo.k.l.ee.er.   v.i.j.u.t.
[Rough justice]R.u.v.   j.u.s.t.i.s.

[Just a minute]J.u.s.t.　u.　m.i.t.i.t.
[Judge and jury]J.u.j.　a.t.t.　j.uu.r.ee.

Chapter 23 - Lip shape Y
[Help yourself]K.e.l.m.　y.uu.s.e.l.v.
[Yorkshire pudding]Y.uu.k.j.u.　m.uu.t.i.ng.
[Yesterdays model]Y.e.s.t.er.t.e.ee.s.　m.o.t.l.
[Usual price]EE.OO.j.ee.oo.u.l.　m.r.a.ee.s.
[Young and beautiful]Y.u.ng.　a.t.t.　m.ee.oo.t.i.v.uu.l.
[Stop worrying]S.t.o.m.　w.u.r.ee.i.ng.
[What a carry on]W.o.t.　u.　k.a.r.ee.　o.t.
[Use the yard broom]EE.OO.s.　th.u.　y.a.t.　m.r.oo.m.
[A lovely holiday]U.　l.u.v.l.ee.　k.o.l.i.t.e.ee.
[Fast and furious]V.a.s.t.　a.t.t.　v.y.uu.r.ee.u.s.
[Fall by the wayside]V.uu.l.　m.a.ee.　th.u.　w.e.ee.s.a.ee.t.
[A secure loan]U.　s.e.k.y.uu.r.　l.o.oo.t.

Chapter 25 - Lip shape OO
[Too good to be true]T.oo.　k.uu.t.　t.oo.　m.ee.　t.r.oo.
[Like a shoe box]L.a.ee.k.　u.　j.oo.　m.o.s.
[Stuck in the groove]S.t.u.k.　i.t.　th.u.　k.r.oo.v.
[Good news]K.uu.t.　t.ee.oo.s.
[I knew it too]A.EE.　t.ee.oo.　i.t.　t.oo.
[It glows in the dark]I.t.　k.l.o.oo.s.　i.t.　th.u.　t.a.k.
[Blow me down]M.l.o.oo.　m.ee.　t.a.oo.t.
[Something to crow about]S.u.m.th.i.ng.　t.oo.　k.r.o.oo.
u.m.a.oo.t.
[I doubt that]A.EE.　t.a.oo.t.　th.a.t.
[Go down town]K.o.oo.　t.a.oo.t.　t.a.oo.t.
[He's browned off]K.ee.s.　m.r.a.oo.t.t.　o.v.
[That's not allowed]TH.a.t.s.　t.o.t.　a.l.a.oo.t.
[Large crowd]L.a.j.　k.r.a.oo.t.

[Nothing to shout about]T.u.th.i.ng. t.oo. j.a.oo.t.
u.m.a.oo.t.

Chapter 26 - Lip shape ER
[Early Bird]ER.l.ee. M.er.t.
[Cold Turkey]K.o.oo.t. T.er.k.ee.
[Stern warning]S.t.er.t. w.uu.t.i.ng.
[Clean shirt]K.l.ee.t. j.er.t.
[Dirty linen]T.er.t.ee. l.i.t.e.t.
[First come first served]V.er.s.t. k.u.m. v.er.s.t. s.er.v.t.
[Early service]ER.l.ee. s.er.v.i.s.
[Silver service]S.i.l.v.er. s.er.v.i.s.
[Beef burger]M.ee.v. m.er.k.er.
[Church service]J.er.j. s.er.v.i.s.
[Give it a twirl]K.i.v. i.t. u. t.w.er.l.
[Happy returns]K.a.m.ee. r.e.t.er.t.s.

[AIR]
[Share and share alike]J.e.er. a.t.t. j.e.er. u.l.a.ee.k.
[Invisible repair]I.t.v.i.s.i.m.l. r.e.m.e.er.
[We're nearly there]W.ee.er. t.ee.er.l.ee. th.e.er.
[Fair shares]V.e.er. j.e.er.s.
[Threadbare armchair]TH.r.e.t.m.e.er. a.m.j.e.er.
[Where there's a will]W.e.er. th.e.er.s. u. w.i.l.
[Ne'er do well]T.e.er. t.oo. w.e.l.
[Stand and stare]S.t.a.t.t. a.t.t. s.t.e.er.
[Upstairs to bed]U.m.s.t.e.er.s. t.oo. m.e.t.
[A breath of fresh air]U. m.r.e.th. o.v. v.r.e.j. e.er.
[Aware of the danger]U.w.e.er. uu.v. th.u. t.e.ee.t.j.er.
[Not a care in the world]T.o.t. u. k.e.er. i.t. th.u. w.er.l.t.

Chapter 27 - Lip shape EE][Lip shape EE

[Eat something sweet for a treat]EE.t.   s.u.m.th.i.ng.
s.w.ee.t.   v.uu.   u.   t.r.ee.t.
[Are you feeling fit?]a.   y.oo.   v.ee.l.i.ng.   v.i.t.
[A square meal.]U.   s.w.e.er.   m.ee.l..
[Has the mail come yet?]K.a.s.   th.u.   m.e.ee.l.   k.u.m.
y.e.t.
[How much does it weigh?]K.a.oo.   m.u.j.   t.u.s.   i.t.
w.e.ee.
[It is time to try again.]I.t.   i.s.   t.a.ee.m.   t.oo.   t.r.a.ee.
u.k.e.ee.t..
[Mind how you go.]M.a.ee.t.t.   k.a.oo.   y.oo.   k.o.oo..
[Too many cooks spoil the broth.]T.oo.   m.e.t.ee.   k.uu.k.s.
s.m.uu.ee.l.   th.u.   m.r.o.th..

Chapter 28 - Lip shape I and II
[Biting wind]M.a.ee.t.i.ng.   w.i.t.t.
[Thin Ice]TH.i.t.   A.EE.s.
[Fighting fit]V.a.ee.t.i.ng.   v.i.t.
[High price]K.a.ee.   m.r.a.ee.s.
[Mild chill]M.a.ee.l.t.   j.i.l.
[Chilly wind]J.i.l.ee.   w.i.t.t.
[In flight service]I.t.   v.l.a.ee.t.   s.er.v.i.s.
[Tight fit]T.a.ee.t.   v.i.t.
[Bright idea]M.r.a.ee.t.   a.ee.t.ee.u.
[Try it on]T.r.a.ee.   i.t.   o.t.
[Fried fish]V.r.a.ee.t.   v.i.j.
[Slight chill]S.l.a.ee.t.   j.i.l.

Chapter 29 - Lip shapes NG
[Spring chicken]S.m.r.i.ng.   j.i.k.e.t.
[Golf links]K.o.l.v.   l.i.ng.k.s.

[Cufflinks]K.u.v.l.i.ng.k.s.
[A willing horse]U.　w.i.l.i.ng.　k.uu.s.
[Soft filling]S.o.v.t.　v.i.l.i.ng.
[Single bed]S.i.ng.k.l.　m.e.t.
[String along]S.t.r.i.ng.　u.l.o.ng.
[Wrong turning]R.o.ng.　t.er.t.i.ng.
[Bring to order]M.r.i.ng.　t.oo.　uu.t.er.
[Things to do]TH.i.ng.s.　t.oo.　t.oo.
[Lip reading class]L.i.m.　r.ee.t.i.ng.　k.l.a.s.
[In the pink]I.t.　th.u.　m.i.ng.k.
[Sprung a leak]S.m.r.u.ng.　u.　l.ee.k.
[To be frank]T.oo.　m.ee.　v.r.a.ng.k.

Chapter 30 - URE
[Buried treasure]M.e.r.i.t.　t.r.e.j.y.uu.r.
[Amateur team]A.m.a.t.y.uu.r.　t.ee.m.
[Insult to injury]I.t.s.u.l.t.　t.oo.　i.t.j.u.r.ee.
[Boring lecture]M.uu.r.i.ng.　l.e.k.t.y.uu.r.
[Life of leisure]L.a.ee.v.　o.v.　l.e.j.y.uu.r.
[In the picture]I.t.　th.u.　m.i.k.t.y.uu.r.
[Endure to the end]E.t.t.y.uu.r.　t.oo.　th.u.　e.t.t.
[Natural causes]T.a.j.er.u.l.　k.uu.s.i.s.
[Future success]V.ee.oo.t.y.uu.r.　s.u.k.s.e.s.
[Securely locked]S.e.k.y.uu.r.l.ee.　l.o.k.t.
[Miracle cure]M.i.r.u.k.l.　k.y.uu.r.
[Curiosity killed the cat]K.y.uu.r.ee.o.s.i.t.ee.　k.i.l.t.　th.u.
k.a.t.
[Manicured nails]M.a.t.i.k.y.uu.r.t.　t.e.ee.l.s.
[It's a pleasure]I.t.s.　u.　m.l.e.j.y.uu.r.

Chapter 31 - Lip shape U and IA

[Under the stairs]U.t.t.er.   th.u.   s.t.e.er.s.

[Upstairs]U.m.s.t.e.er.s.

[London Underground]L.u.t.t.u.t.   U.t.t.er.k.r.a.oo.t.t.

[Curry powder]K.u.r.ee.   m.a.oo.t.er.

[All above board]UU.l.   u.m.u.v.   m.uu.t.

[Dental Appointment]T.e.t.t.u.l.   A.m.uu.ee.t.t.m.e.t.t.

[Cup of coffee]K.u.m.   o.v.   k.o.v.ee.

[Custard powder]K.u.s.t.a.t.   m.a.oo.t.er.

[Apple crumble]A.m.l.   k.r.u.m.m.l.

[Utter rubbish]U.t.er.   r.u.m.i.j.

[Uncomfortable ride]U.t.k.u.m.v.t.e.ee.m.l r.a.ee.t.

[By all appearances]M.a.ee.   uu.l.   u.m.ee.er.r.u.t.s.i.s.

[Bus pass]M.u.s.   m.a.s.

[Untrue story]U.t.t.r.oo.   s.t.uu.r.ee.

Chapter 32 - Lip shape UU

[Put your foot in it]M.uu.t.   y.uu.   v.uu.t.   i.t.   i.t.

[Could you come]K.uu.t.   y.oo.   k.u.m.

[Little choice]L.i.t.l.   j.uu.ee.s.

[Choice of words]J.uu.ee.s.   o.v.   w.er.t.s.

[More choice]M.uu.   j.uu.ee.s.

[Oily rag]UU.EE.l.ee.   r.a.k.

[Foot in the door]V.uu.t.   i.t.   th.u.   t.uu.

[Good morning]K.uu.t.   m.uu.t.i.ng.

[Food for thought]V.oo.t.   v.uu.   th.uu.t.

[Short fuse]J.uu.t.   v.ee.oo.s.

[Claw back]K.l.uu.   m.a.k.

[Good book]K.uu.t.   m.uu.k.

[Good look]K.uu.t.   l.uu.k.

[Calling card]K.uu.l.i.ng.   k.a.t.

13. Lip shape Master Copies

Two copies of each lip shape are provided the larger shaded version should be used for creating you lip shape library.

The smaller unshaded version is provided so that you can try out your own shading or colouring of the images.

The collection contains a number of alternative lip shapes that do not appear in the Lip Shape Text samples. They are:

K+a, K+e, K+m, K+oo, K+r, L+ee, L+oo , NGa and NGb

You should refer to the section on Alternative Lip Shapes for information on how to use them.

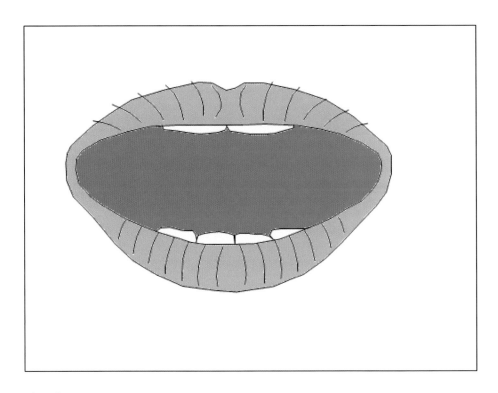

Lip shape A

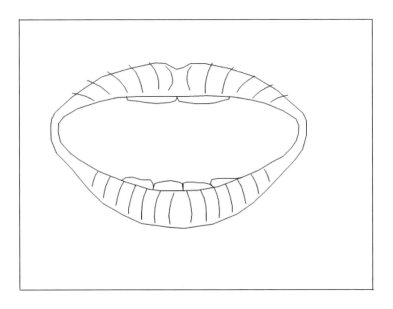

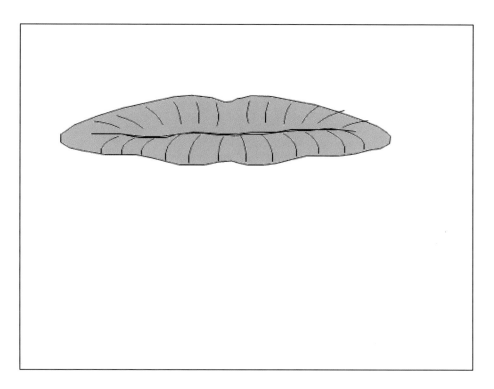

Lips at rest

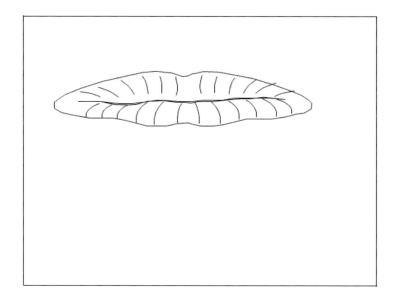

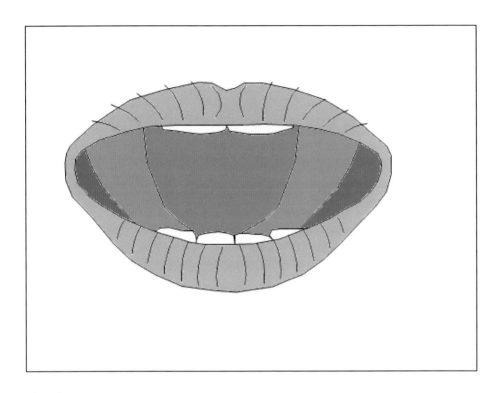

Lip shape E

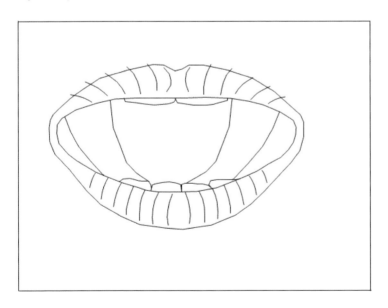

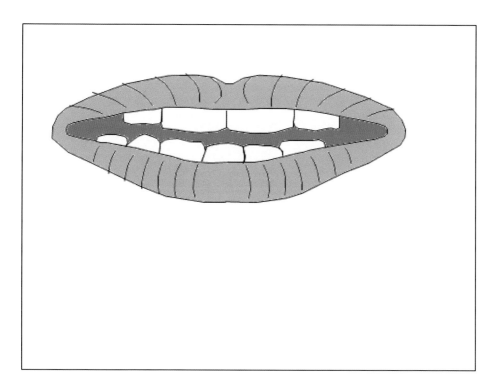

Lip shape EE

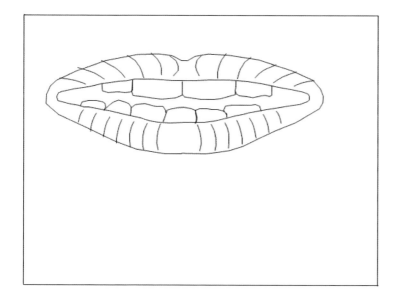

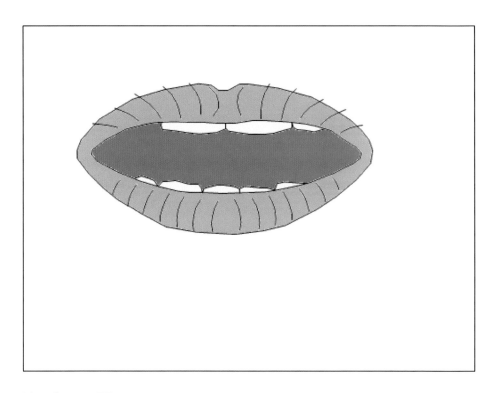

Lip shape ER

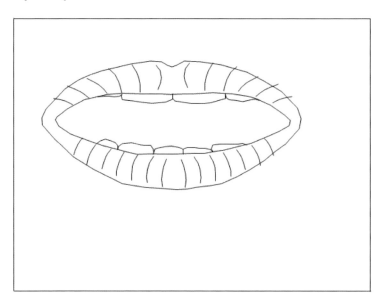

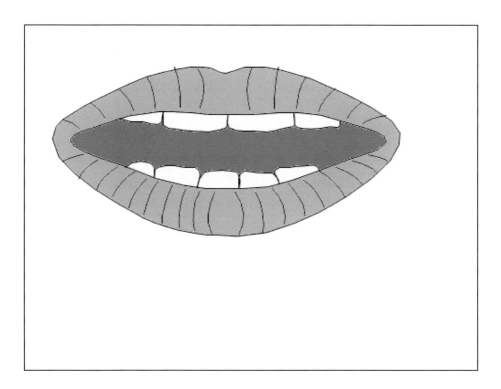

Lip shape I

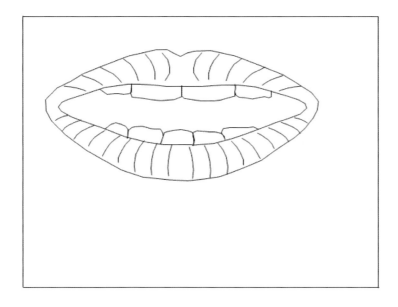

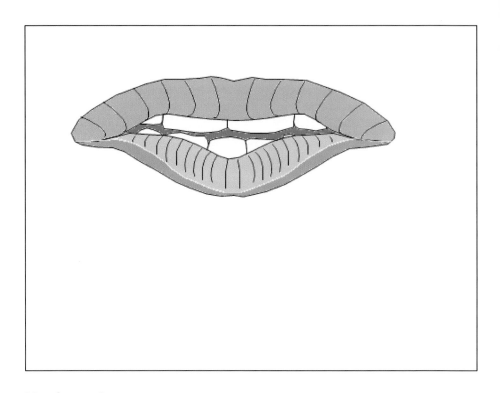

Lip shape J

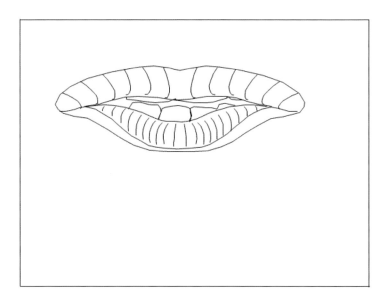

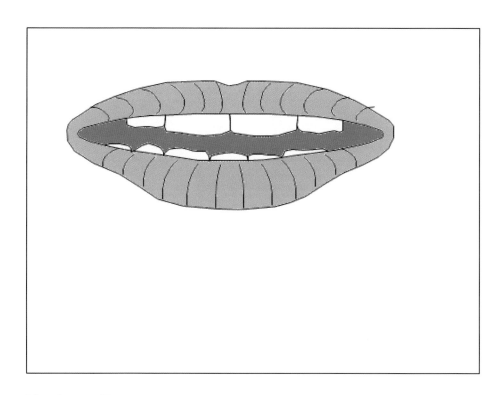

Lip shape K

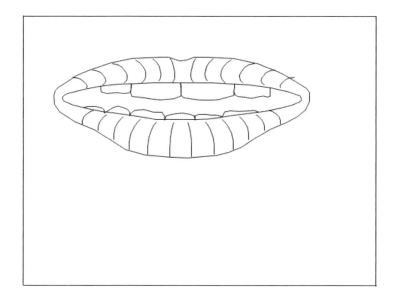

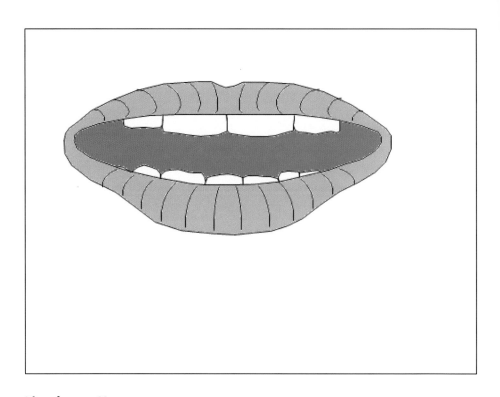

Lip shape K+a

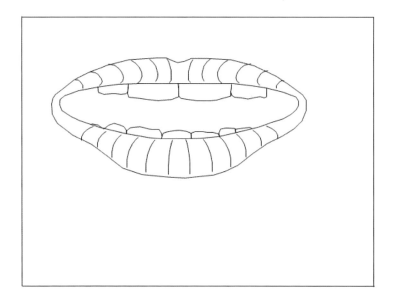

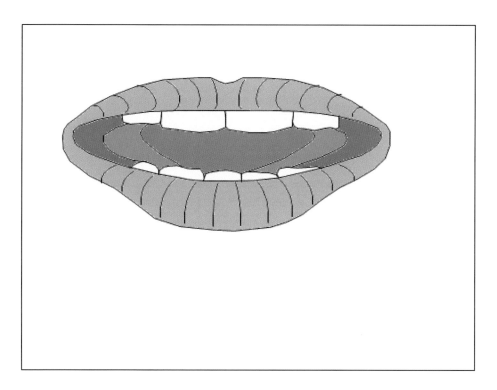

Lip shape K+e

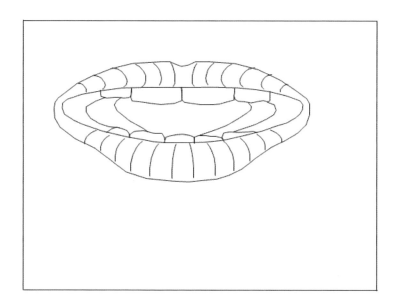

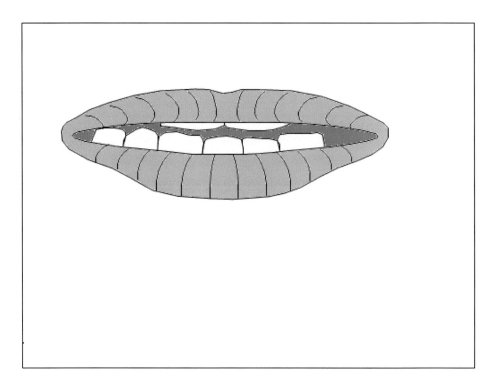

Lip shape K+m

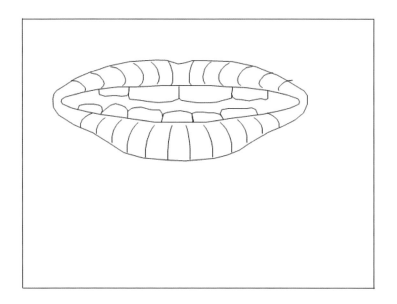

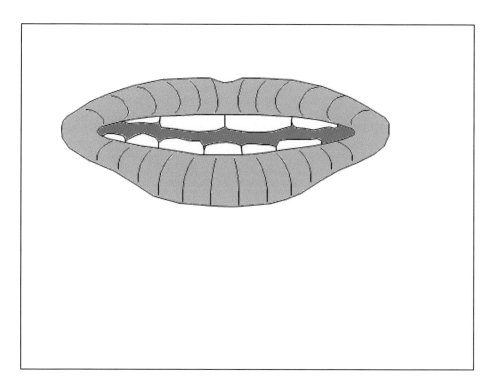

Lip shape K+oo

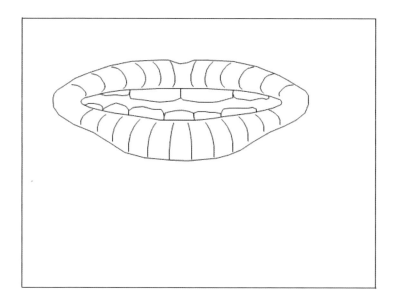

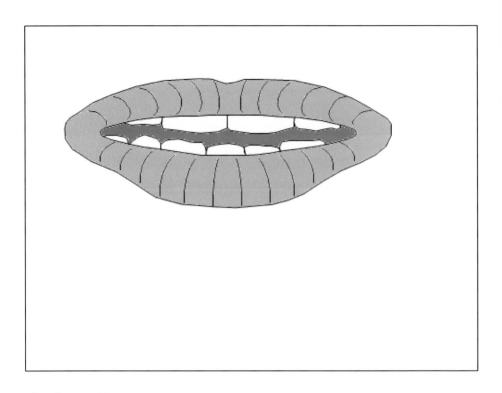

Lip shape K+r

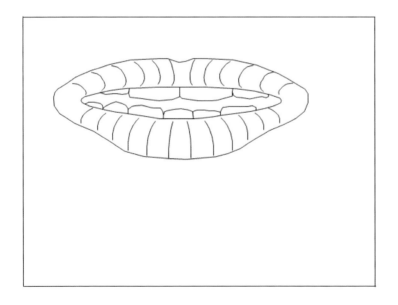

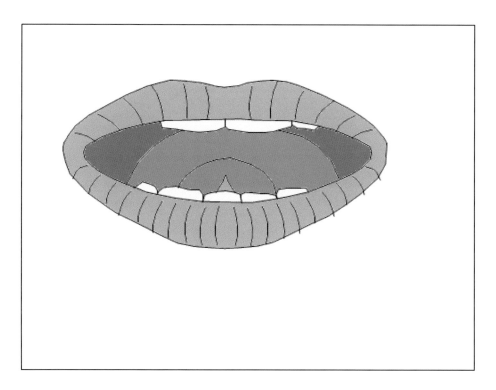

Lip shape L

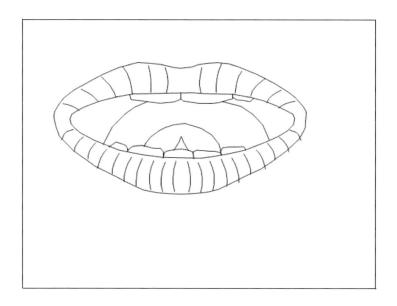

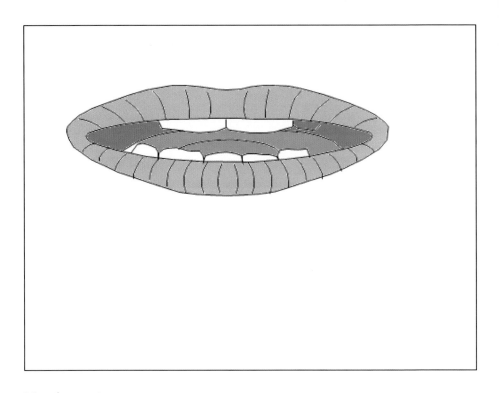

Lip shape L+ee

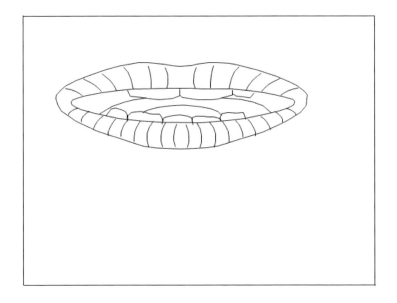

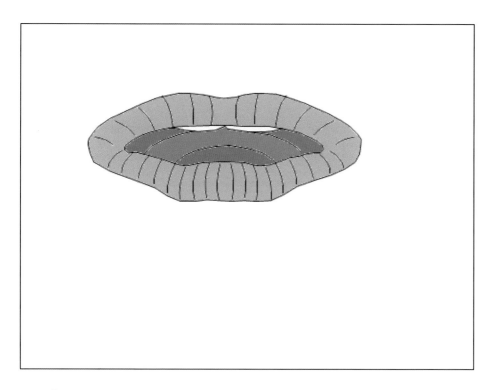

Lip shape L+oo

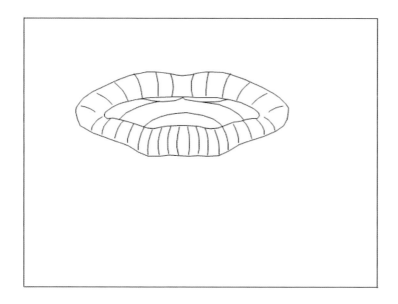

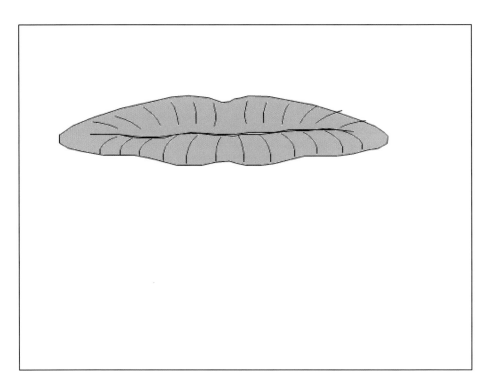

Lip shape M

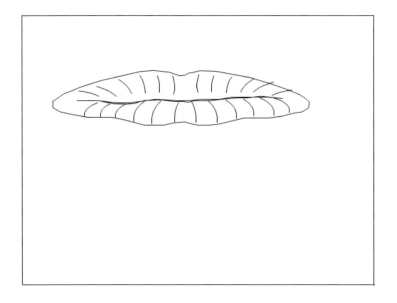

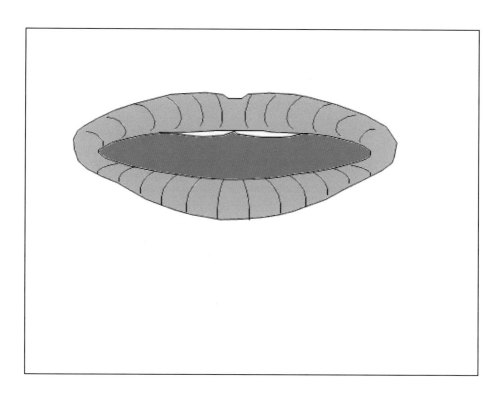

Lip shape NGa

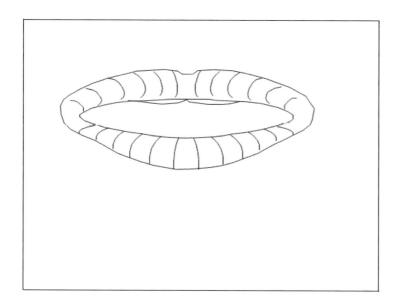

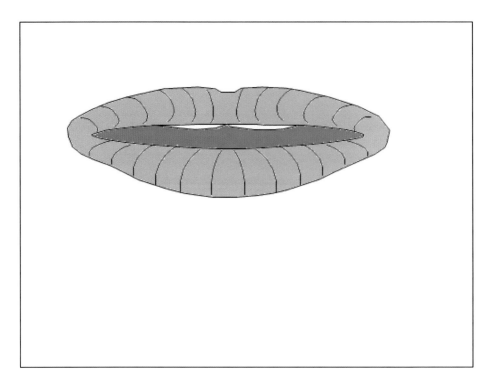

Lip shape NGb

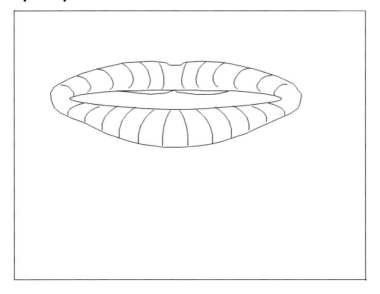

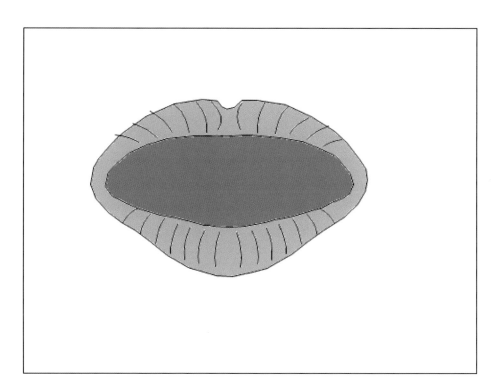

Lip shape O

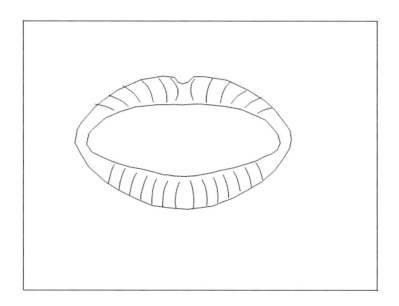

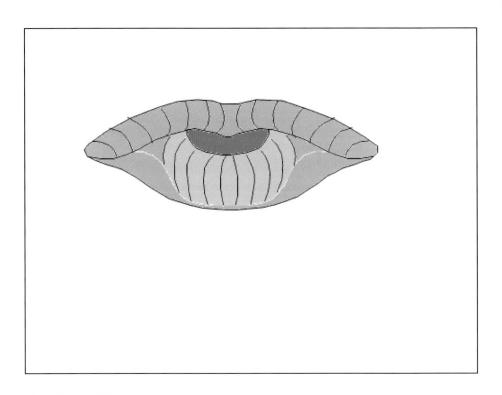

Lip shape OO

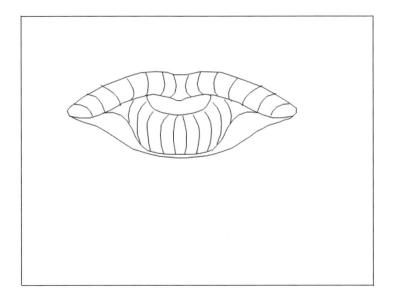

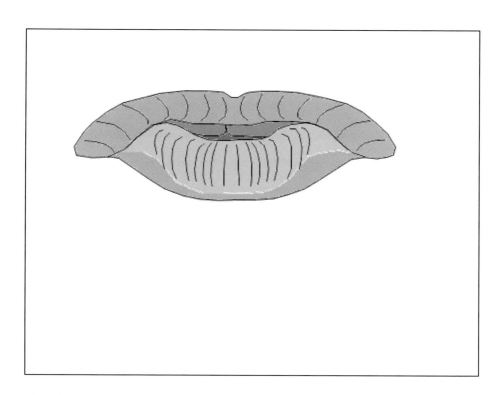

Lip shape R

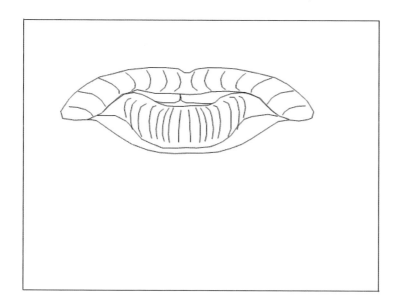

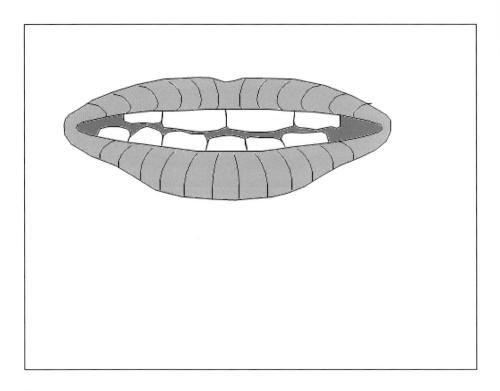

Lip shape S

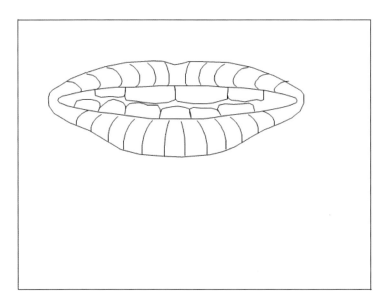

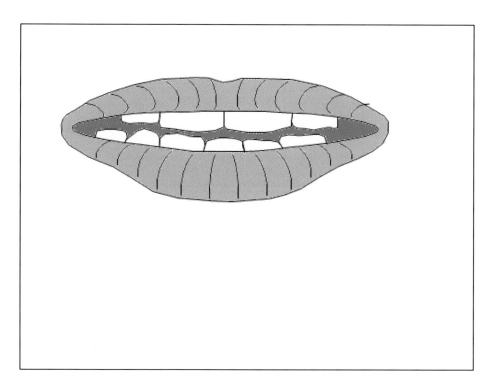

Lip shape T

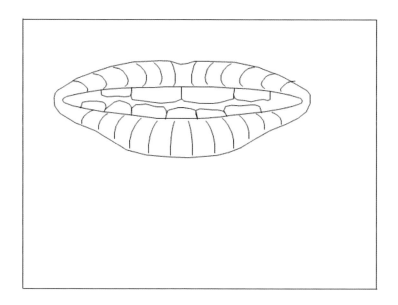

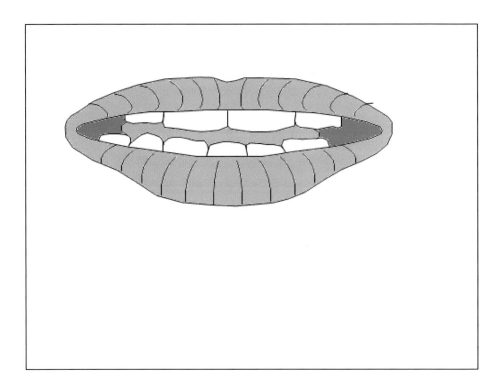

Lip shape TH

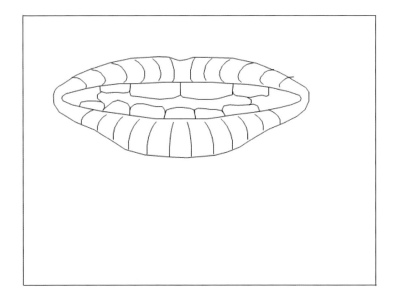

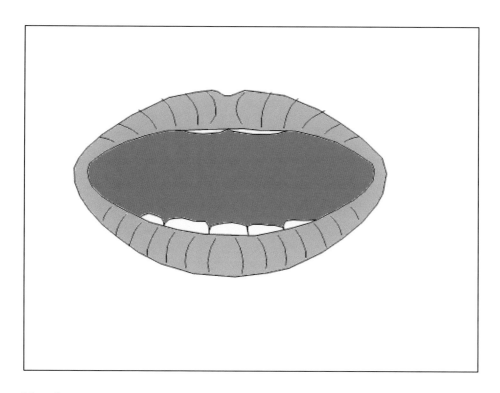

Lip shape U

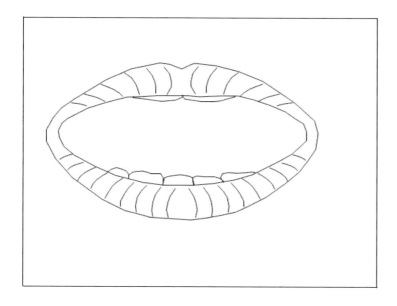

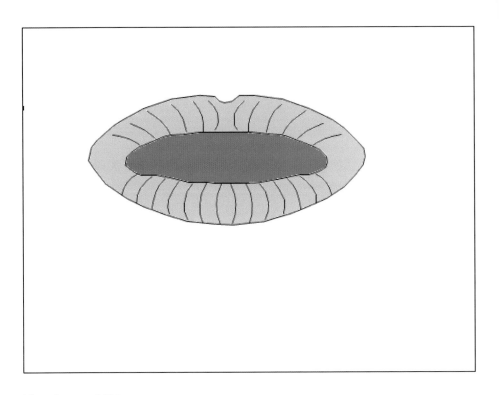

Lip shape UU

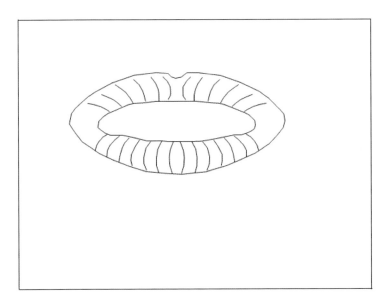

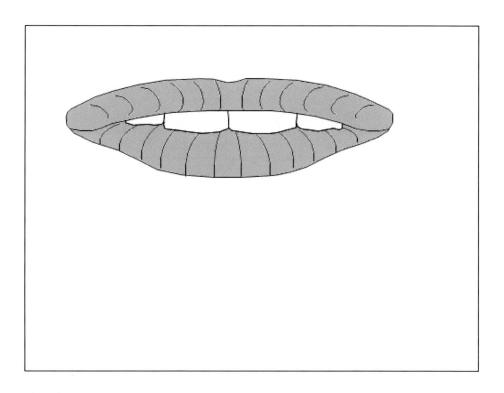

Lip shape V

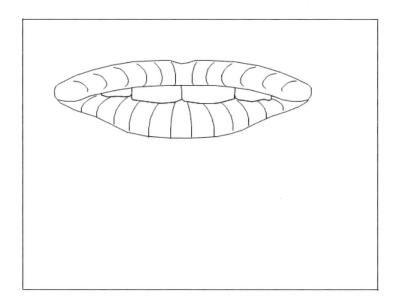

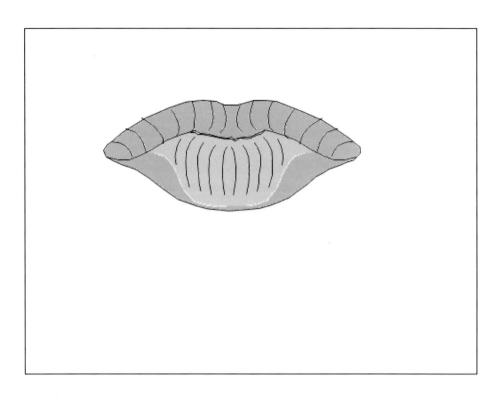

Lip shape W

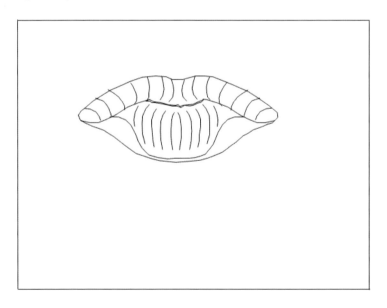

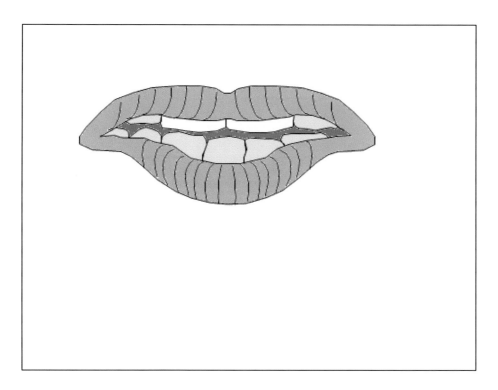

Lip shape Y

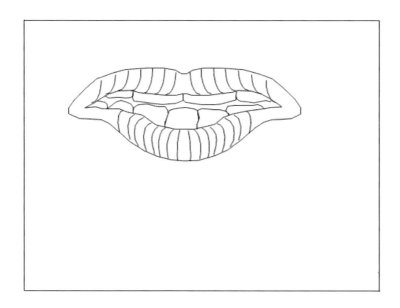

14. Table of Phonetic symbols and sounds:

A as in hat	**N** as in nail
AH as in car	**NG** as in Thing
AIR as in care	**O** as in Hot
AW as in claw	**OH** as in Crow
AY as in hay	**OI** as in Boy
B as in box	**OO** as in Cool
C as in cat	**OW** as in Cow
CH as in choice	**P** as in Post
D as in dog	**Q** as in Queen
E as in tent	**R** as in Rat
EAR as in clear	**S** as in Silver
EE as in feet	**SH** as in Ship
ER as in hurt	**T** as in Tiger
EW as in few	**TH** as in thick
F as in Fig	**U** as in cup
G as in goat	**URE** as in pure
H as in hot	**UU** as in foot
I as in lip	**V** as in vast
IA as in idea	**W** as in wax
II as in cry	**X** as in box
J as in jam	**Y** as in year
L as in list	**Z** as in zoo
M as in make	**ZH** as in decision

Phonetic text uses the above symbols to represent the sounds of speech instead of using conventional spelling.

15. Phonetic text to lip shape conversion table:

Phonetic Symbol	Lip Shape(s)	Phonetic Symbol	Lip Shape(s)
A	A	N	T
AH	A	NG	NG
AIR	E.ER	O	O
AW	UU	OH	O.OO
AY	E.EE	OI	UU.EE
B	M	OO	OO
C	K	OW	A.OO
CH	J	P	M
D	T	Q	W
E	E	R	R
EAR	EE.ER	S	S
EE	EE	SH	J
ER	ER	T	T
EW	EE.OO	TH	TH
F	V	U	U
G	K	URE	Y.UU.R
H	K	UU	UU
I	I	V	V
IA	EE.U	W	W
II	A.EE	X	S
J	J	Y	Y
K	K	Z	S
L	L	ZH	J
M	M		

16. Primary lip shapes:

Lip Shape **A (hat)** for A, AH and OW1	Lip Shape **E (tent)** for E, AY1 and AIR1	Lip Shape **EE (feet)** for EE, AY2, EW1, IA1, II2 and OI2	Lip Shape **ER(hurt)** for ER and AIR2
Lip Shape **I (lip)** for I	Lip Shape **J** for CH, J, SH and ZH	Lip Shape **K** for C, G, H and K	Lip Shape **L** for L
Lip Shape **M** for B, M and P	Lip Shape **O (hot)** for O and OH1	Lip Shape **OO (too)** for OO, EW2, OH2 and OW2	Lip Shape **R** for R and URE3
Lip Shape **S** for S, X and Z	Lip Shape **T** for T, D and N	Lip Shape **TH** for TH	Lip Shape **U (cup)** for U and IA2
Lip Shape **UU (put)** for AW, OI1, URE2 and UU	Lip Shape **V** for F and V	Lip Shape **W** for Q and W	Lip Shape **Y** for Y and URE1

17. Sliding Lip Shapes – the lips change from the first shape to the next shape while the sound is being made:

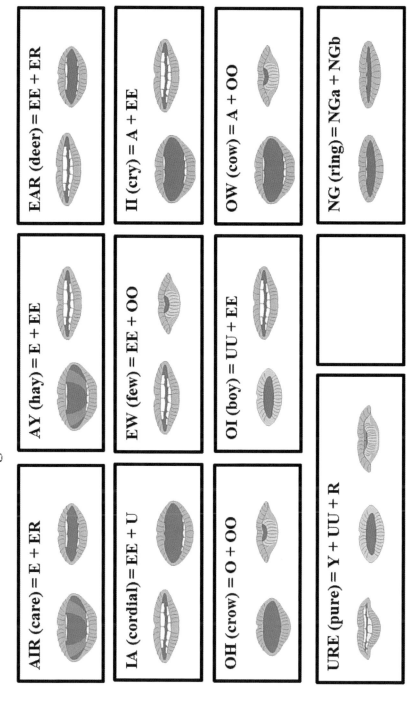

AIR (care) = E + ER

AY (hay) = E + EE

EAR (deer) = EE + ER

IA (cordial) = EE + U

EW (few) = EE + OO

II (cry) = A + EE

OH (crow) = O + OO

OI (boy) = UU + EE

OW (cow) = A + OO

URE (pure) = Y + UU + R

NG (ring) = NGa + NGb

18. Alternative Lip Shapes

The collection of Lips Shape master copies has a number of extra shapes that do not appear in the samples of lip shape texts used to construct the animations.

They are as follows:

K+a, K+e, K+m, K+oo, K+r, L+ee, L+oo , NGa and NGb.

If you examine these lip shapes you will see that they are modified versions of lip shapes K, L and NG.

The companion book "Lip Reading - self-help textbook" describes the three consonants in some detail and you should refer to that book for a full explanation of why these extra lip shapes are required.

The intention here is to show how these extra shapes can be used in your animations to obtain smoother and more realistic representations of speaking lips.

NGa and NGb

The NG sound is made as the lips move from lip shape NGa to lip shape NGb. So whenever lip shape text spells NG you should put NGa followed by NGb into your animation.

L+ee and L+oo

The L sound is made inside the mouth and does not rely on lip shape for its production. So provided the lips are parted the L sound can be made. In most cases when we say L the lips make lip shape L as included in the master copies. But where the L sound is accompanied by the vowel EE or OO one the alternative versions (L+ee or L+oo) should be used. It doesn't matter whether the EE or OO vowel precedes or follows the L, the alternative version is the one to use.

K+a, K+e, K+m, K+oo and K+r

The group of sounds associated with lip shape K (C, G, H and K) are even less dependent on the specific shape of the lips for their quality of sound. Provided the lips are parted the sound can still be made. What happens in speech is that when we make any of the sounds in the K group the lips take on a shape that is close to the lip shape of the adjacent vowel. So when assembling the lip shapes for your animation, if K is preceded or followed by A, use lip shape K+a. The result will be a more smooth and natural animation.

Table for use of Alternative Lip Shapes:

Lip Shape Text	Alternative Lip Shape sequence	Lip Shape Text	Alternative Lip Shape sequence
A.K	A.K+a	**EE.L**	EE.L+ee
K.A	K+a.A	**L.EE**	L+ee.EE
E.K	E.K+e	**OO.L**	OO.L+oo
K.E	K+e.E	**L.OO**	L+oo.OO
M.K	M.K+m	**NG**	NGa.NGb
K.M	K+m.M		
OO.K	OO.K+oo		
K.OO	K+oo.OO		

Printed in Great Britain
by Amazon